KNOWINGLY LEADING

'25 Conversations for Leadership Success'

Author:

Doug Booker

Copyright © 2012 Doug Booker

All rights reserved.

ISBN-10: 1503047946
ISBN-13: 978-1503047945

TABLE OF CONTENTS

INTRO & PURPOSE	2
_____	
1-GET REAL FAST	14
2-VISION	19
3-CREATING YOU	26
4-TEACH FISHING	36
5-ETA	43
6-FOREVER TRUST	51
7-INDIVIDUAL FIRST	62
8-NON THREATENING	68
9-THOSE OTHERS	75
10-BOTTLENECKS	82
11-NEWBIES	91
12-WHO YOU ARE	97
13-MORE TRUST	103
14-EVALUATION	113
15-FAMILY	125
16-MY WAY	130
17-CONSENSUS	137
18-TURNOVER	143
19-CHANGE	149
20-CONFLICT	157
21-ISSUES WITH U	165
22-FINE LINE	170
23-BAD APPLES	176
24- ROOT CAUSE	181
25-TOP 10 NEEDS	185
_____	
WRAP UP	193
AUTHOR / BOOKS	196

ACKNOWLEDGMENTS

The learning expressed within this book is dedicated to all those I have learned with - since my Leadership Journey began in earnest, two or three decades ago!

*"There are quotes, phrases and pictures/graphics found within that I have found in places since forgotten. No intent here to plagiarize or otherwise use someone's creativity w/out permission. Where I know who to give credit – I have (I hope).

Purpose & Introduction

The bottom line reasoning and purpose for this book is to *finally* provide how 'I would do it' for leaders. Many leaders struggle and lack executing important, transparent and real dialogues with individuals - as well as their teams. The 25 conversational-topics here are to help leaders successfully relate and therefore lead! I can also assure you that IF you execute and pursue the intent of these vignettes, you will also be *teaching* leadership – not just doing it!

If you are searching for an academic or theoretical resource on management, you will want to put this back on the shelf. This is a *conversationally* written book on application and practicality. This is a HOW TO, not a WHAT IS resource.

Those who know me realize I coach, teach, facilitate and consult in a very Socratic way. That questioning way of mine led to the focus of my first book 'Teaching Fishing for Managers'. After a couple of decades and books planting seeds and encouraging leaders to think - I have decided to provide *my* answers and thinking. This is a plan of success for those in leadership roles, from CEO to front-line supervisors. If you lead a group of people at any level this *will* work. You *will* be KNOWINGLY LEADING!

Getting us started here, I *will* ask just this one question,
    "Why do you believe you are leading; how do you know?"

KNOWINGLY LEADING!

If you are unsure; open to not knowing the answer to this question; or are simply still growing and learning - this book will be invaluable. If you are just beginning your leadership journey, this is your guidebook to success with people. Undoubtedly you will march past peers who are not having these conversations (and not creating effective relationships).

I am not trying here (as I did in other books) to create awareness or convince you of the value and critical importance of LEADERSHIP. I am assuming you have this book in your hands to simply 'continually improve' your own leadership; and to grow those you lead.

In these past decades of working with leaders, I have learned much and realized much about the challenges leaders face in 'leading'. For the most part, what I have learned – again, was shared in my previous three books on Leadership (see last few pages of this book for information).

*If you would like a (free) eBook/PDF version of any, just let me know!

I have little doubt that combining this book's content along with the messages of the others (books) will place you in very good stead as a leader.

This book is 'me telling you' the conversations that I would have with those I lead - leadership according to Booker!

These are specific actions, communications and behaviors that will lead you to becoming 'an effective leader'. You DO all this and you will be KNOWINGLY LEADING.

This will happen by intentionally and sincerely having conversations and following through on the *intent* of these 25 leader-to-follower talks (developing trust and relationships)

Here's what I know: IF you DO these talks in your first months of assuming a leadership role (and continually come back and reinforce them), you won't be calling me or some other Leadership expert down the road when things go badly?!

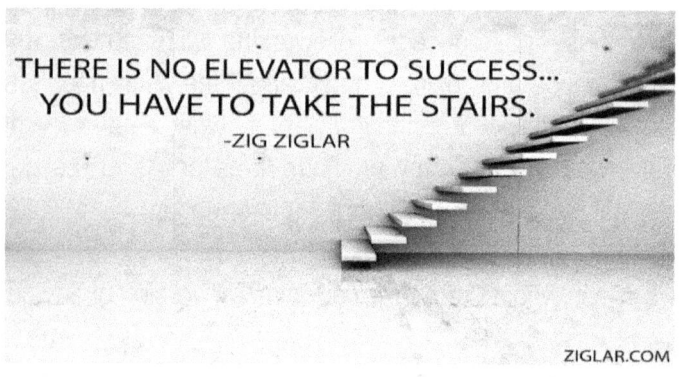

IF you are picking this (book) up and implementing the talks in the middle of things (after being on the job/in the position for some period of time), then regardless, START NOW! Holler at me if I can help steer your efforts. There may be some bumps in the road you need to think through if you haven't been really practicing these concepts previously.

So it's simplicity-time. What follows is a strategy for KNOWINGLY LEADING - 'walking that talk' of which we have all heard; and few of us have experienced.

YOU are the leader here. Internalize the intent first and then go talk to 'these 25' in any way that best fits you, your personality, your style, etc. Take the time to truly capture the meaning of each vignette and see the vision of what they will create. Then do that NIKE-thing, JUST DO IT (talk, converse, listen, discuss and improve things, repeat, etc).

If I can help you work through the 'how to', feel free to pick up the phone and call me to discuss – sincerely! (My contact info is in back of the book). My passion is to help leaders lead …here if I can help you my friend.

These talks are written from the point of view of the leader. These are not talks for bellowing out to the masses, but rather between leader and his/her followers (and team). These are concepts to work out with each individual you lead - as well as the team you lead.

If you are leading a group and wish to grow YOU and them, this is your book. This is for the CEO and his/her ELMT (Executive Leadership Management Team) – the team at the top. It is also for the supervisor of a group of operators on the front line.

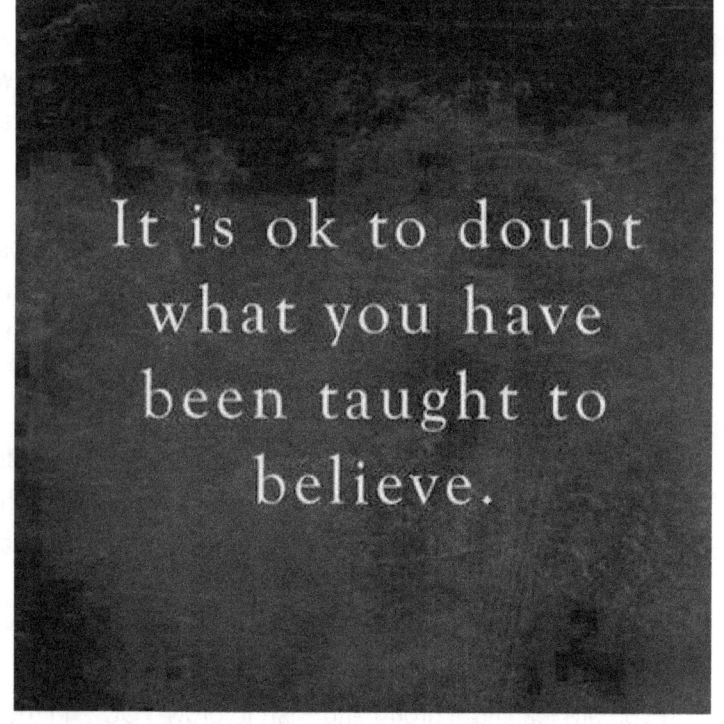

So let's get into it, changing you and your leadership for the better, likely way better! Here goes...

❖ **GET YOUR THINKER GOING!**

These are some thoughts about what many leaders walk into upon assuming a new management role; these would be my assumptions and beliefs going into any leadership situation:

(ASSUMPTIONS):

- Leadership may not have been effective previously. Some have really never experienced leadership.

- Bad relations & conflict likely exist w/in your sphere; on your team and around you. (Likely between your predecessor, your new Dept/team and other players throughout the organization).

- On your team are *dominators* (we know what they look like huh?). There are also *cavers* (people who don't speak up but quietly/non-productively exist on the team waiting for another day to end).

- Distrust is present (on this team) with management. Because I *am* management, (even though they never laid eyes on me) – they don't trust me either. I may not have caused their distrust, but it is my problem now.

- Likely maybe as little as 30% of the team does most of the inputting, deciding, talking in meetings and thinking.

- CONSENSUS is a much under-utilized concept; likely never really practiced effectively (to say the least).

  - My boss likely is not a great leader and is from the same dysfunctional leadership-development world from which most in management were birthed. I will have to discuss and maybe 'upwardly coach' him/her on all these conversations/dynamics.

- Relationships between my office & other departments & divisions of the company may not be good.

  - Feedback, input, evaluation, coaching and people-development has been ineffectively executed (to say the least).

  - Presently, people are NOT our most valuable resource. People's minds & hearts - are not used to their fullest and therefore are a much wasted asset.

(RECOMMENDATIONS):

- Read, ponder & embrace these 25; spend time here in these talks - digesting their intent, challenge and value.
- Do not move forward w/out YOU understanding and thinking through these first. YOU must *buy-in* first.

- You maybe (likely) have no real mentors/trusted advisors. Find mentors to help you with this.

- Make these 25 YOURS!!! This will not be the last time I mention this. Adapt, add, edit, and change my conversations here, to your own style without losing the message.

- Along the way, discuss each of these with (coach-up ☺) your boss.

- Involve your subordinates (individual and collectively) with your intent. Maybe even give them a copy of these 25 after the first few conversations?

- Create accountabilities to hold yourself to, in making all this real – involve others as accountability-partners.

- Remember the adage about 'only being as strong as your weakest link'. Do not try to move forward with any of these 25, without everyone on board. You took time to buy in, allow them to buy-in and be part of the vision. (By doing things this way, you will be practicing that consensus-thing, FYI).

- New people will have to be brought on board (with all these messages) as they show up on your team over time. Plan for them 'getting' these messages (the /ways of your new culture).

❖ **<u>OK REALLY, A FEW LAST REMINDERS</u>**

These vignettes are captured and presented in various ways. Some are dialogues somewhat laid out as I would say them. Some are writings about topics I am suggesting you put into your own words and then speak to them. In some cases I am clearly just sharing some writing on the point for you to chew on and spit out in your own uniquely transparent way. Admittedly some are a bit 'confusingly written' requiring a bit of thought and work on your end. Digest, think and maybe do other research on the topic and point.

Within each vignette you will see discussions (DISCUSSION:) to the left margins. To the right, there is <u>underlined dialogue</u> – justified to the right margin. The concept here is the discussions are there for directly facilitating, teaching or even reading with/to your people and team. The underlined information to the right is sort of just my *admin* direction, thoughts and guidance to YOU about what's happening. You'll see. Once again, it is all YOURS. Maybe you will discuss all (to include the underlined words).

One last time - get the *message and intent* deeply into YOU first. There are topics of critical importance here; you have to create the conversation personal to YOU THE LEADER and your situation.

Regardless, the point to all this is - have the freakin' conversations!!! These must become who YOU are. You will then be KNOWINGLY LEADING! You will be also growing new leaders. You will be teaching 'leadership' as you work through these (you'll see).

These talks are for the leader who is willing to be transparent, vulnerable and maybe even naked – exposing her/his soul to the team. These are for the leader who has come to realize real relationship comes from being real. It (leadership & relationship) happens when YOU are willing to abandon all the management nonsense, buzzwords, gimmicks, programs and myths. Clearly this takes a secure leader, insecure ones will never pursue this...

Are you tired of doing nothing, or maybe tired of wasting time and money on useless short-term fixes to LEADERSHIP, TEAMERSHIP and RELATIONSHIPS?

Read the entire book, study all conversations first. Then create your plan and strategy for how you will sequentially approach all.

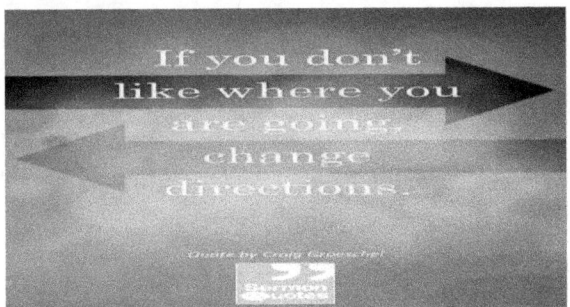

> *I do want to mention that these (and many other pertinent leadership principles) are what I teach and preach in my business (www.bookertraining.com); if I can help you in facilitating some or all of this, call to discuss.*

LEADERSHIP WISDOM

"...Blessed is the man who finds wisdom ...and gains understanding." PROVERBS 3:13

"...He who loves discipline loves knowledge; he who hates correction is stupid..." PROVERBS 12: 1

"The way of a fool is right in his opinion, but the one who listens to advice is wise." PROVERBS 12: 1

KNOWINGLY LEADING!

1
GET REAL, FAST

(PRETENDING TO BE A LEADER IS A WASTE)

DISCUSSION: I want to be real here with you all ...this team I am here to lead. I am not perfect; I will need you and let me say right up front, I want to share some assumptions I have as we begin this journey....

KNOWINGLY LEADING!

<u>Possibly write these on whiteboard before or during the discussion?</u>

DISCUSSION: Some assumptions I make here and now:

- I am not a great leader; you get to determine that during our journey. Likely I am only 70% of what I could/will be.
- This is not a great team; we are likely functioning at about what - maybe 70% of our real potential, huh?
- I can only lead effectively with help from you and others.
- Relationship and Trust must be our priority.
- You (and I) have possibly never seen effective leadership and great relationships on a team?

Your thoughts?

<u>You may wish to include other ASSUMPTIONS I listed above in Purpose/Introduction…</u>

<u>A critical piece of your overall success will depend on the quality and 'real-ness' of this/future talks. Are you real and transparent? Do you let them go first?</u>

DISCUSSION: I want to know who you guys are, your stories, where you come from, likes & dislikes. ….and anything else you want to share? If you are open to it, how about telling us one thing that nobody here knows about you? Think this is kinda hokey don't you?...

<u>Get to know them FIRST before imposing who YOU are, all your credentials and why you are so wonderful.</u>
<u>Let them talk about 'them', individually and collectively. This is you setting precedence of your Servant Leadership attitude – you are here for them, not vice versa.</u>

<u>Keep this positive and assure them you (we) will start working on us – you, me, the team, etc… shortly (upcoming conversations in this book).</u>

<u>"Go Team" and other rah-rah speeches are useless in the beginning. They have heard them before – and most likely they never transpired.</u>
<u>Once again, just be real and talk to them face to face, same level, and maybe sitting vs standing.</u>
<u>Despite all the management speak (myths) you have heard, you do want/need them to like you.</u>

DISCUSSION: I want to share with you my favorite quote and tell you why it is...

"People don't care how much you know until they first know how much you care!"

- Experience has taught me this is true.

- What I believe kills most in management (not getting this).

- I want you to hold me accountable to practicing this.

- Most of my past leaders have believed 'knowing more, being right', etc is their source of power. They were wrong...

- ....more?

TALK #1 THINKING:

- ❖ **Takeaways**

- ❖ **Issues I need to think through and discuss with mentors**

- ❖ **What did Booker really intend here**

- ❖ **What do I want to add**

- ❖ **What are my concerns with this topic**

2
THAT VISIONING TALK

(BUT NEVER USE THE WORD 'VISION')

(Review Assumptions listed on page 8)

DISCUSSION: I want to re-visit and further discuss some more assumptions which I believe exist; I want your input regarding them? I realize there is a fair amount of dis-trust surrounding us at this very moment.

I am hoping for but not totally expecting great dialogue right here right now ...because of that distrust...?

So here's a question for you. IF we can improve us to become an awesome team in maybe 3 - 6 months from now, what would this perfectly awesome team look and feel like? What do you/we want us to be?

<u>Do not interject YOUR words, thoughts or traits. It is CRITICAL that this be 'their' vision (teaches servant leadership, consensus, they matter, etc)!</u>

<u>Be OK with quiet, pause, thinking, apathy ☺ ...be persistent until you get maybe 12, 15 or 20 descriptors. I am betting your list will resemble something like this list:</u>

supportive, caring, helpful, respect, family, clear roles, relationships, no conflict, teamwork, fun, on the same page, communicates, work ethic, fair, everyone does their job, accountability

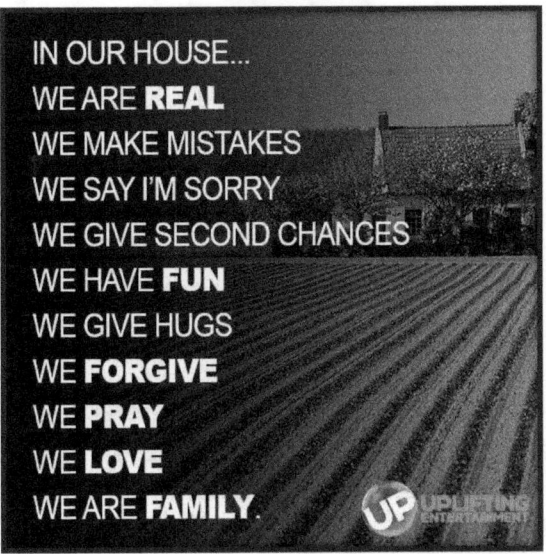

DISCUSSION: So as we look at the list of words you gave me about what you want us to be; how would you rate this team right now on a scale of 1 to 10? Using your words up on the board as your criteria, and with (1) being 'really bad' and (10) being 'perfect team stuff' – how do you rate us currently?

<u>Have everyone give a number; might be a good idea to get them to write it down before sharing out loud. Maybe additionally seek their experience (in their adult worlds with teams), what's the average rating of all those teams?</u>

<u>Press them to be honest; likely you will initially get some inflated numbers. They are not ready yet to completely dump on themselves/this team. Realize that in all likelihood whatever # they do give you, that number is actually lower…?!! They are just afraid to say it right now.</u>

<u>After seeking and getting input, summarize/average out the results and put that number (betting it is maybe around 7.0?</u>

<u>I also bet if you asked them in an environment of total trust, that number would be more like 6.0 (you will get there☺). If the numbers are really high, you have some significant trust issues to work through yet. Don't fall into the trap of believing you walked into this simply awesome team that's a 10! You didn't.</u>

<u>It is still early and relationship and trust do NOT exist yet; but maybe the following can be pursued a bit right now:</u>

DISCUSSION: What would it mean if we could go from a 7.0 (their number) to an 8.0? Speak of how this is all just about *continuous improvement* of your most valuable operating system – our/your, this team and our People System!

What would it take, or how could we get there?

<u>Pursue some quality conversation; it may not be all comfortable. That's a good thing – learning that we only get better by working through the discomfort!</u>

<u>Near the end of this conversation, make this point:</u>

DISCUSSION: You realize what all these words and thoughts mean huh? You have just created our VISION. That's the vision I (along with all of you) are now accountable for, because it is what YOU said YOU wanted; all of you/us. Now I have to lead us to get there with your help; it is on all of us, beginning right now, to begin policing ourselves and each other. This will require us catching ourselves when we are not BE-ing these words - to change our behaviors and create this culture.

I want to emphasize a point here, since it is how I want to be as a leader. We (you) created this VISION, not me. I practice consensus in my way of leadership and I want you to know this – we will make decisions as a team. Hold me accountable to this if you see me doing otherwise.

<u>You may have to have some initial discussion of 'consensus' here. (More on CONSENSUS in future conversations here in the book).</u>

<u>Throughout these initial discussions in the early days, be ready for lots of rolling eyes and apathetic comments and non-verbals. They have heard all these 'TEAM rah-rahs and GO TEAM speeches' before...</u>

Either you or a volunteer or two might take this list and create some kind of visual to plaster around the place with wording or a title maybe like 'OUR VISION, WHAT WE WANT US TO BE, WHAT WE SAID WE WANT, WHAT WE ARE, WILL BE, WHERE WE ARE GOING, BE THIS, etc.

Maybe email the list to all...

(You get the idea. It becomes a visual accountability which in never-ending fashion, you should always point individuals and the team back to in discussions.)

Additionally you may want to send it to each/all in an email asking for feedback about the conversation, the list, accountabilities, etc…

OK, so that is one of the first conversations to have with the team. Important point here (take note), never mention the word 'visioning' until the conversation is over! Most people have seen many useless efforts regarding visioning. Don't let them know they are creating one (vision) until they have – the list on the board is IT! Now go turn that vision into their (your) reality.

How? …continue these talks!

TALK #2 THINKING:

- ❖ Takeaways

- ❖ Issues I need to think through and discuss with mentors

- ❖ What did Booker really intend here

- ❖ What do I want to add

- ❖ What are my concerns with this topic

- ❖ What might I need to discuss with my leader/boss?

3

CREATING THE LEADER

(THAT'S YOU)

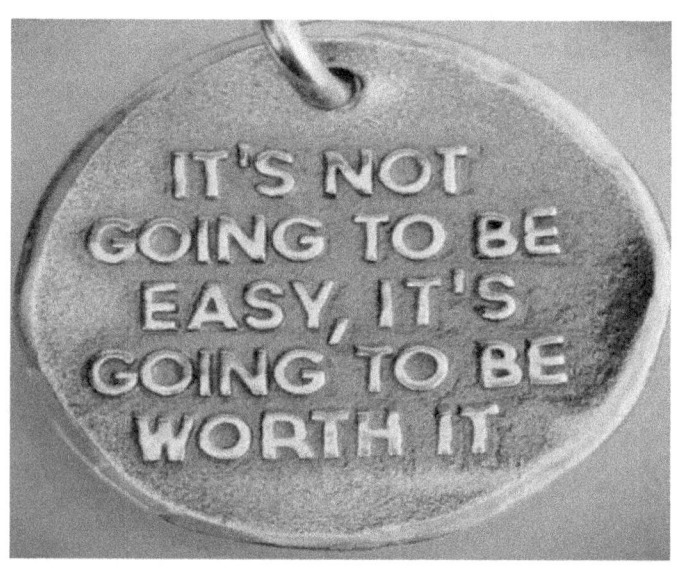

<u>This is another critical piece or conversation; maybe the very most important one!</u>

<u>It is the one that will absolutely set the tone for every day of your future. Think through this and do it well. Keep tying things together, as you do this conversation, tie it back to the vision and those words</u>

KNOWINGLY LEADING!

(after you brainstorm here and get their LEADER QUALITY words on the whiteboard).
Make the connection for them.
Also remember that one of the underlying goals (which is a *word* in your vision) is to create TRUST. Every conversation needs a focusing first by you on the trust dynamics...

DISCUSSION: Any thoughts on the VISION discussion we had the other day? Are we any better yet? Anything happened at all good or bad in regard to getting closer to that vision?

Don't expect much. However, for the rest of your life with them, keep this conversation on the horizon; find ways to apply and connect the vision they created to how you do business....

One way of making that vision happen is tied to this second vignette.

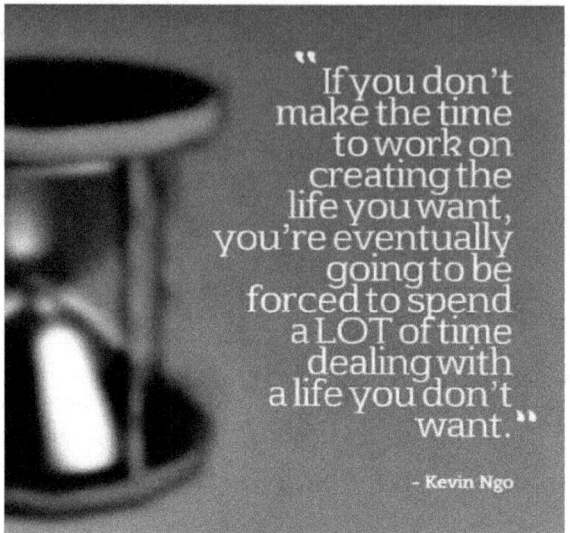

<u>Write the words 'LEADER QUALITIES/TRAITS' in the center of whiteboard.</u>

DISCUSSION: I want to take us though some thinking regarding me, your leader. I am the one on the hook to facilitate us achieving the vision, the culture we all said we wanted here. So how do I grow me? How do I know if I am leading effectively? How does anyone know he/she is leading? What is a good leader? What is leadership?

<u>Give them some time to think and spout out some thoughts about your questions above.</u>

KNOWINGLY LEADING!

DISCUSSION: These are the beginning questions to us improving ME and my leadership, relationships and teamership here in our division. To begin with, let's do a bit of brainstorming...

On a piece of paper, take maybe 2 minutes and write down the qualities, traits, characteristics that make an effective leader to you? Think of this any way you wish: describing what a great leader you are☺, a famous leader, bad leaders and capture their 'opposites', coaches, etc. This is your list, what is important to you in a leader? What do you want in me? OK go ahead...

<u>Now get their words up on the whiteboard for all to see, likely some 15-20 words is the goal. It will likely have some connection and resemble the VISION list. (They should, that's a good thing – *think about it*)</u>

<u>Now talk them through the following writing (give them a copy maybe):</u>

DISCUSSION: Let me read this piece called 'The Leadership Dilemma' (an article I borrowed). This is written by a Leadership & Management Consultant I know.

.....In organization after organization that I work with, in assisting them in the development & improvement of their 'people-system', I discover the same common Leadership Dilemma. The company is attempting to improve productivity, solve quality issues, resolve conflict and / or increase profitability with untrained leadership and management.

People who know their stuff and are experts of sorts, but who have never been mentored/trained regarding LEADERSHIP! Repeated over and over, it's the same ol' story: An individual is there for a long time, has done a great job, and knows all the technical aspects – operations - services…so surely he/she will be an effective leader?!

SURPRISE!!!!,……..it rarely works out that way, does it?!?

Here's a more typical outcome: this new leader (who has been told subconsciously that he/she has been promoted for what he/she KNOWS - suddenly discovers that being a supervisor is not so easy after all. "My technical know-how doesn't seem to get me anywhere with these people. They don't seem to appreciate me being in their face telling them how to do their job (which by the way, I call 'coaching, mentoring and bottom line, sharing my wisdom)…hummmm? Additionally, I seem to now have a lot more people-problems and no one cares about mine! What's going on…nothing seems to work with this unappreciative and unmotivated bunch!"…..sound familiar?

Before long, this previously cooperative, dependable and knowledgeable employee (now turned supervisor) becomes public enemy #1 to his/her people. Threatening, intimidating and hollering becomes the preferred communication technique. "Why don't they just do what I say and respect me...after all, I am their boss!" There is a lot of mumbling and grumbling about how you have forgotten where you came from and who your friend's are/were. "I am not a bad person, why isn't this working?".....consider this quote as part of the solution:

"People don't care how much you know until they first know how much you care!"

In many ways, this same dynamic is the same one that challenges small businesses, and small business owners/managers. Think about it, once again people are attempting to lead with a skill-set that is all about the 'technical/operational' knowledge of whatever service we provide or product we make! Management is all about the product/service, with no regard for the importance and relevance of leadership and management concepts. Once again, the leadership, people skills, managerial concepts, etc are the 'assumed' skills and qualities that are only considered well after-the-fact, when things begin to go badly. More than likely, these dynamics will only truly come to light after the initial burst of success that the business experiences....after much growth, which everyone gets excited about, with all the dollars rolling in....

'Thinking' that challenges leaders:

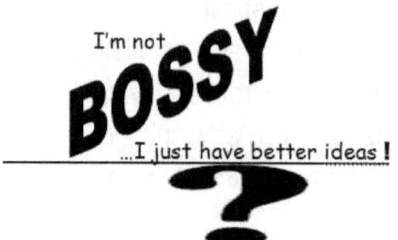

Slowly but most certainly, the owner/manager begins to realize that there is more to running a business/organization than producing a product or providing a service!!! Once again the awareness of this comes way too late in the game. Relationships are damaged, ...roles have become blurred, ...conflict is everywhere, ...people don't want to come to work (much less work for you!), ...loyalty dies, ...customers are unhappy, ...mumbling and grumbling is occurring and most of this muttering is directed at YOU!!! It is for all this logic and reasoning why I feel compelled to push the following quote on management:

<u>Write this quote on the white board:</u>

"People don't care how much you know until they first know how much you care!"

DISCUSSION: You have seen this before huh? I spoke to it our first day. How am I doing regarding this quote?

Let's think about it and its application here with us/me. What got me here, is not what will take me into the future successfully.

How does this relate to me and my development as your leader? How does it apply to your thinking about yourself and leadership in general?

<u>Share with them; be transparent and let them see what a difficult challenge this is for anyone to be a leader...</u>

<u>Down below is a handout (WHAT THEY ALL SAY), which I always give to each 'after' they commit and create their own list on the whiteboard. Let them experience the similarities and you make the point - it's what we all want in our leader huh?</u>

DISCUSSION: So again, how do I BE all this? We have to create accountabilities that you all can hold me to, to change/improve my behaviors.

<u>Discuss this list/handout and how it connects to the words 'they' put on the board. What's the message to you and to them about growing YOU?</u>

<u>Q: Don't the competencies of the leader need to be aligned with our VISION (words the team created earlier)?</u>

What they all say!

> "A top 20 listing of what hundreds of groups of supervisors, managers and executives have identified as the traits they want in leaders; what last 2500 people said! Look kind of familiar?"

Involves & asks my opinion

Cares

Understanding & Patience

Open-minded

Honest & Trusting

Fair & Consistent

Listens & Informative

Respect

Clear Directions / Expectations

Supportive & Helpful

Works with Me

Coach / Teacher

Motivates & Inspires

Firm & Decisive

Problem-Solver

Dependable

Individual & Team-builder

Shields & Protects

Role Model & Sets Example

KNOWINGLY LEADING!

TALK #3 THINKING:

- ❖ **Takeaways**

- ❖ **Issues I need to think through and discuss with mentors**

- ❖ **What did Booker really intend here**

- ❖ **What do I want to add**

- ❖ **What are my concerns with this topic**

- ❖ **What might I need to discuss with my leader/boss?**

4
TEACHING FISHING

(THAT 'ONE THING' THAT WILL CHANGE YOU)

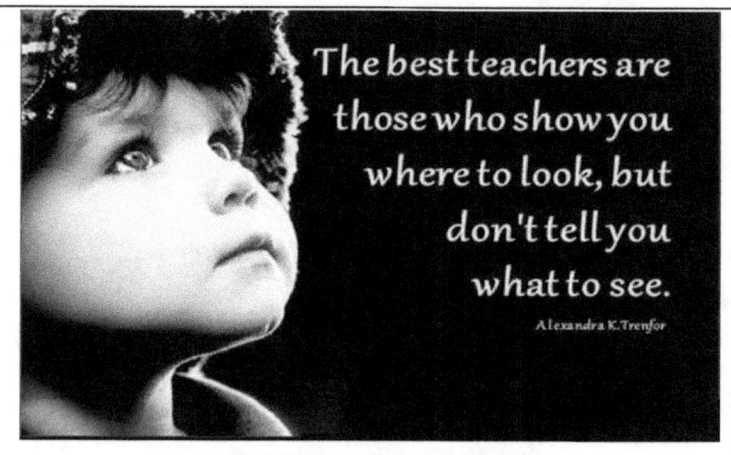

···as well as THE BEST LEADERS···

<u>This vignette is in the front of the book, at the head of the list of conversations for a reason.</u>

<u>The concept here/below is the 'one thing' I have come to believe that answers the question, "what is one thing that will make me a better leader?"</u>

KNOWINGLY LEADING!

<u>I tell leaders to master this if they want to change and improve their own leadership. From your first day with a new team, group or department of people - use this skill and you will BE about:</u>

consensus, involving people, seeking the best idea, team problem-solving, developing people, two heads are better than one, respect, them vs you leadership, servant leadership, upward communication, etc.

<u>However you choose to talk to, internalize or share about this concept - lead with some words such as:</u>

DISCUSSION: I do not want to be a dictating, directing or 'telling' leader. I want to be one that facilitates and works with you to solve problems, to learn with, etc. I want to be a servant leader; one who serves the team in leader-ly ways; not someone who micro-manages or tells you how to do your job. That's your job – to do your job huh?

I want to be a facilitator. When you ask me for answers and solutions, count on me to come back first with something like, 'what would you do?'

Hold me accountable to do things this way with each of you.

Below is a quote / phrase that may or may not be familiar to you but regardless, don't discount it too quickly as just another quote. It has 'extremely' deep roots related to my potential success as a LEADER!

Give a man a fish
And he eats today....
Teach a man to fish and
He eats for a lifetime

In the past I used to mutter these words below. A zillion times I found myself in this discussion or conversation with other leaders and managers:

"...day after day, I have people lined up at my door or catching me walking around, wanting to know this or that? ...what to do about this? ...how to handle that? ...and on and on and on and on and on and on it goes"

(You get the picture, right?) Now go back, let's read the 'fishing' quote above, and see if we see any application or connection? You see, the trap we fall into as leaders (and most of our teachers did as well) is in attempting to handle this and handle that, answer this, solve that, provide a solution here and tell them how they should deal with this or that.... When we do this, we are just 'handing out fish'.

KNOWINGLY LEADING!

(Is the picture getting more and more familiar to you…do you recognize this trap?)

This is an interesting dilemma I had pointed out to me – I was told:

'Now don't beat yourself up too quickly here. To begin with, this is a good thing about YOU. Our instinct is to do the right, helpful and leader-ly sort of thing here - help them out with an answer. That's good right? No, that's bad and you have already determined why, haven't you?'

There is another real-life issue that causes us to fall into this trap; it's called TIME! (It's very efficient to just give answers rather than getting your people to think. Annnnnnd the quicker that I give him an answer, the quicker I can GIVE THE NEXT PERSON A FISH. And besides, isn't that my job as the leader to do the THINKING anyway? OK, ALL together now:

"Oh no, all I am doing is providing fish instead of TEACHING PEOPLE TO FISH FOR THEMSELVES!!!" Now ask yourself this question: "Where will these same people come the next time they are hungry?"

OK gang, so here's the TIP OF THE DAY for us: LEADERS, MANAGERS, PARENTS or TEACHERS: I want to develop the habit that when people come to me with problems or questions, I respond with:

> When you talk, you are only repeating what you already know. But if you listen, you may learn something new.

- WHAT WOULD YOU DO?
- WHAT DO YOU THINK?
- HOW WOULD YOU DO IT?

My first book 'TEACHING FISHING FOR MANAGERS' is a short read that goes into this habit/skill extensively.

Here is a free eBook/PDF version of the book, copy/paste into your browser:

KNOWINGLY LEADING!

http://goo.gl/2KnwX1

***Printed version can be found on Amazon or contact me directly for purchasing a copy.**

*PART II of this book goes into great depth how to understand and master the skill of 'teaching fishing'...

TALK #4 THINKING:

- **Takeaways**

- **Issues I need to think through and discuss with mentors**

- **What did Booker really intend here**

- **What do I want to add**

- **What are my concerns with this topic**

- **What might I need to discuss with my leader/boss?**

5

EXPECTATIONS, TRUST & ACCOUNTABILITY (ETA)

(YOUR EVERY RELATIONSHIP WILL IMPROVE)

C OMMITMENT
A CCOUNTABILITY
R ELATIONSHIPS
I NTEGRITY
N EVER STOP LISTENING/LEARNING
G OLDEN RULE

Write the three words 'EXPECTATIONS, TRUST, ACCOUNTABILITY' on a whiteboard as you begin…

DISCUSSION: Think about these three words (expectations, trust and accountability) for a minute and see if you have a thought about how they work together in terms of relationships?

I suspect that you are beginning to piece them together somewhat. I think you will agree that the following usage of these concepts is a good foundation for any leader at any level.

Moreover, any two people in a relationship of any sort, would do well to practice this between them as well. Let's get into it; this is what I want all of our relationships to BE with each other!

EXPECTATIONS: This is the beginning and yet, more often than not, ends up being the ending that leads back to the beginning. Confused?...I'm not sure what I just said either!

Put it this way: in the working relationship between a leader and his/her people, 'expectations' is where much time should/needs to be spent—but oftentimes is not.

<u>You may want to point out its value to the players on a team as well. Each of them with their co-workers, peers, teammates...</u>

DISCUSSION: ...and ohhhh how we pay for it when we *assume* rather than spend the time communicating and clarifying what is expected. Both parties need to make sure that this time is committed to....pay me now or pay me later.

What is the expected outcome? What is the standard? How much authority is granted? What are the milestones or deadlines? Is there a need for coaching and feedback sessions as we go? How will we measure success? How much experience and capability does the individual possess?

TRUST: Once the expectations ARE established, clarified and agreed upon—trust becomes a significant player in the process. There are trust issues with both parties that need to be understood, discussed and practiced. Trust is developed in both directions when expectations are clear, feedback is open and we accomplish the tasks at hand. But trust can be stressed and ruined depending on how both leader and follower behave during the process.

Consider how trust is potentially violated: the leader violates it when he/she constantly checks, micromanages, asks questions on the status, looks over the shoulder, etc.

The follower breaks it (and we all have) by not completing it, and possibly worse than that, bringing it to the boss two minutes prior to deadline stating that they cannot get it done...and boy is the follower getting ready to be held accountable!!! And he/she should be, huh?

Now the boss is on the hook and ultimately responsible and there is no way out for him....

So things turn ugly, and what's the result? Trust and the working relationship is severely eroded regarding future efforts, overall work and situations that arise.

ACCOUNTABILITY: This phase (of ETA) can be either good or bad, fun or not, depending on the outcome. I can hold you accountable by chewing your #!@*.... praising your good job... recognizing failure and ensuring we learn from it....etc, etc, etc.

Typically, when things go bad....it all leads back to a lack of time spent on the front end on EXPECTATIONS. There must be clarity on the front end---open, honest relevant words regarding this delegation or assignment of duties.

Was the follower comfortable enough to ask questions in the initial phase or along the way? Was the leader available? Did we provide him/her with the authority to get it done? Important and necessary questions.

If we practice this process (E-T-A), correctly and effectively, the result will likely turn out in a very expected manner. It doesn't mean we won't fail; but we will learn and maintain the working relationship!

More thoughts to practice and teach about ETA:

DISCUSSION: In speaking to a friend sharing good news about moving up and assuming a new management role, we discussed 'starting right'. I shared that in many ways, the success factors' are the same for any of us entering a new role with new people (leader or not). While especially critical for the leader – the following is critical for any of us, anywhere at anytime IN THE BEGINNING. These dynamics, thoroughly understood and practiced will undoubtedly get you off on the right foot:

RELATIONSHIPS, EXPECTATIONS & ACCOUNTABILITY

RELATIONSHIP: This is kind of blunt, but here goes: while you are ignorant and stupid about the new situation, job, organization, business, etc, …build relationships!!!. While you are being forced to learn the technical/operational aspects of the biz, get to know people who touch you and your team – in all directions (360degrees around you).

This has been you in your initial days, weeks and months…

DISCUSSION: Discover and uncover 'the inefficiencies and problems' they have or feel about the past as it relates to your position and/or your team. This all pertains to all key players in all directions; the people/team you lead as well as your boss. Do not let any of these players (in your new world/sphere) be anything but a new, positive, caring and *developing* relationship. You must intentionally go make this happen, because it won't just naturally.

<u>As I frequently state it in my coaching– 'go have a cup of coffee with someone before you need them' (hopefully you get the point with this).</u>

DISCUSSION: ....again, while I am learning the biz, I am trying to keep building each and every one of these relationships.

<u>Last point here – do not end up a couple of months later (when you are expected to now 'know stuff') with any relationships headed anywhere but UP! Intentionally focus on this in first months...</u>

DISCUSSION: Of course, everyone won't be easy to do this with, but it is MY choice to make it right. A bit challenging, yes, but what else am I going to be doing while I am overcoming being ignorant and stupid IN THE BEGINNING?

How many of us have ended up in poor, ineffective, unproductive &/or insane relationships simply because these factors were not addressed from the start? How many of us walked away just considering it to be a personality conflict?

DISCUSSION: How am I doing with each of you? Some of us are not where we ought to be; work with me on this will you?

Maybe 'call out' the ones you know YOU are struggling with…

TALK #5 THINKING:

❖ *Takeaways*

❖ *Issues I need to think through and discuss with mentors*

❖ *What did Booker really intend here*

❖ *What do I want to add*

❖ *What are my concerns with this topic*

❖ *What might I need to discuss with my leader/boss?*

6

'TRUST' FOREVER

(TRUST IS NOT A GIVEN. TRUST ME)

TRUST

The knowledge that you will not deliberately or consciously take unfair advantage of me. That I can put my situation, problems, opinions and self-esteem in your hands with confidence.

Loyalty to each other is highly valued and is a top priority to each of us.

<u>A TRUST EXERCISE</u>: Write the number 268 (or some other #, something in the mid-200s) somewhere and keep it hidden preferably away from you somewhere in the room. Have this done before your team enters the room, to be revealed later…

Ask someone to be the recorder for you after writing '500 at the top of the whiteboard and 1 at the bottom'. Give him/her the guidance about when, after each person guesses a number, you will say 'HIGH or LOW'. If I say too HIGH, you write the number up just below 500 (then we are now guessing between their guess and the no#1, get it?) and we will work our way until we get it…

DISCUSSION: I have a number in my head between one (1) and five hundred (500). Anyone know what it is?

Bear with me, this stupid exercise has a point. I have asked (Bob) to record for us, when someone guesses, I will say HIGH or LOW....

So let's begin, who has a guess?

<u>They will begin guessing and you will respond with HIGH OR LOW until someone guesses it. One thing that helps in causing distrust to arise (which is what you want in this exercise) is to do some pausing and hesitating when responding. This causes them to think maybe you are changing the number ☺</u>

<u>(Someone finally guesses it)...</u>

DISCUSSION: OK, so we got it. How did we get there?

<u>Quick dialogue about their ideas about maybe teamwork, involving others, two heads are better than one, etc. (These are great concepts but not the focus of this conversation. Our focus here is TRUST – the point of this exercise as well).</u>

KNOWINGLY LEADING!

DISCUSSION: So what do you think the real point to the exercise is?

<u>Lead them to think through it, maybe even suggesting the question of where that number came from? Someone typically will bring up some point connected to 'trust'.</u>

<u>"How do we know you didn't change the number, huh?"</u>

DISCUSSION: Before anyone got here today, I had that number in my head and never changed it. Do you believe that, YES or NO?

...OK so let's do this, let's take a poll. Who says YES you believe me, or votes for LIAR because you don't?

<u>Write the following on the board:</u>

YES _____
LIAR _____ ☺

<u>They will try to discount their doubting as not calling you a liar, but press them... Yes if you cannot take my word, then you must be accusing me of being a liar.</u>

<u>*In my 15 years of doing this exercise it typically is about 60% calling me a liar! Have fun with this. Don't let it become a self-esteem issue for you; the reality is, we don't trust in our society any more.</u>

DISCUSSION: Talk about issues that lead to distrust:

- Experiences in life being lied to...
- Burned too many times...
- I don't give trust until it's earned...
- You paused/hesitated in saying HIGH or LOW - so you must be lying... (really? ...maybe just slow and stupid at math ☺)
- Relationship, I don't know you well enough yet...
- You are a leader/manager, and I don't trust them...

How does trust play into things right here, right now in this team meeting?

<u>(Show them the number you hid earlier at some point here...stress the point that we have to prove our trust to most people these days...)</u>

<u>I use this point to begin conversation of how people don't talk in groups, having been laughed at, etc. Some will suggest they just like to listen. After suggesting that to be a bunch of #*!@,- nobody comes out of the womb wanting to be alone...</u>

<u>I tell my kindergarten story here to make the point about how we are all impacted to some degree in terms of participating in team/group settings...</u>

> **RESPECT IS EARNED.**
> **HONESTY IS APPRECIATED.**
> **TRUST IS GAINED.**
> **LOYALTY IS RETURNED**

DISCUSSION: Before going on, let me share with you a story of 'learning' and well let's call the key player in story, Susie. This might just be called the story that led to the fallacy many try to spout about no question is stupid. Yes, there is absolutely a stupid question, and we all have asked at least a few of them – leading to at least part of the problem with learning today.

This principle is about how we do this learning-thing so wrong in so many ways from Day ONE in our early seasons of life. (By the way, if Susie is someone's name here, lets change the 'Susie' in the story)?

Go back to or at least try, to day one of your kindergarten class. Picture the setting– boys in new jeans, girls in new dresses, wired and excited about all the stuff they have been told about. They have been pumped up about learning new things, meeting new friends, doing fun things, etc. Got it?

They are all ready, all 20 little knuckleheads (just a term of affection for all of us on this earth☺). All are getting ready to experience their first real taste of TEAMS and LEARNING....

So here it begins; the teacher asks the first question.

Remember this is the first question in the first hour of your very initial experiences with LEARNING and TEAMS.

And here is where it all begins to unravel – the value (and fun?!?!) of SCHOOL, GROUPTHINK, LEARNING, TEAMWORK, etc. Here is where your 'significance' as a Learner began to take shape.

Back to that first question; teacher now unknowingly begins to start messing them up in their learning quest. The kids are wired and excited as they all think they know the answer.

So a question for you: how many raise their hands? Think about it, not as you are now, but as you were way back then, before you learned what you now know – (the abuse people can take in group settings when they attempt to respond, offer a thought, an idea, a solution...)

You are absolutely correct, likely ALL of them raise their hands because they do not know what you and I know. This is not going to be FUN for the person who gets chosen and has the wrong (stupid) answer huh?

Teacher calls on Susie. Susie proudly throws out her best response, what she believes to be THE answer, only to find

KNOWINGLY LEADING!

out, this is something she doesn't understand, didn't learn yet, picked up somewhere erroneously, whatever...

Regardless, she is WRONG.

With this wrong answer, what do we all know occurred in response (from the team mind you)?

She was laughed at, as natural reaction by many, and probably by a few because they are just mean (already).

Teacher, (like most in leader roles, with little to no real understanding of leading, facilitating, or the impact of such a thing on Susie's future life) just allows the reaction. Susie is demoralized while teacher encourages the kids to get quiet, back under control, and teacher moves on...

Now, what do we know about Q#2? Right you are again, Susie ain't playin' no more and neither is anyone sharp enough to figure out already that getting laughed at if you are wrong isn't fun. Not knowing the right answer has now become a threat, an opportunity to look foolish, to be laughed at, and heaven forbid, to be wrong. There is a stupid question (or answer) and I just gave it, thinks Susie and others.

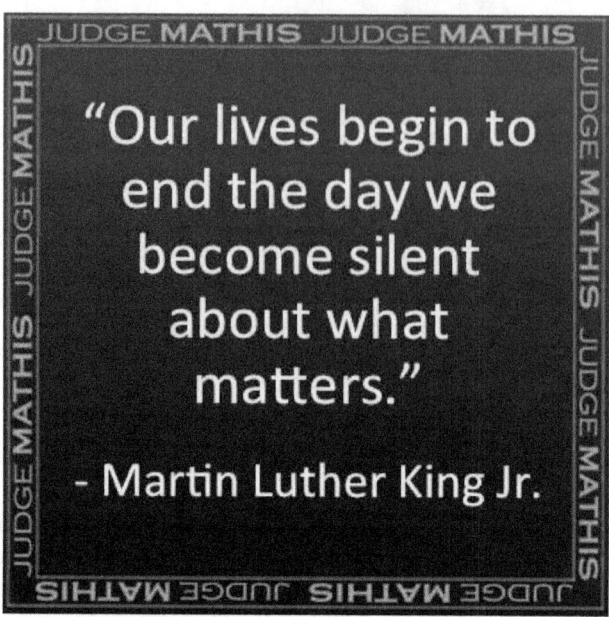

<u>I would normally go forward through the years here in explaining the impact and Susie's continued journey of moving into the 'cave of learning', but will just let you consider that on your own.</u>

DISCUSSION: This was just the first day of the rest of her life (and others like you and I) who were impacted by this throughout our entire school career.

At the end of Day ONE, how many hands were still going up?

A few, maybe, let's say about 15-20%. These are the people, and you know them from your school experience as well as your work world experience; that will be in any/all conversations.

They are the ones who won't be left out of anything, the talkers, and dominators even. Before we leave the end of the first day, picture the interaction between 3-4 kids and the teacher as the others have gone into their safe caves.

<u>That number (15-20%) has an amazing correlation to most all 'teams' in our society's workplaces, adult classrooms, group meetings, etc. On most teams, sad to say, there is usually about 15-20% that do all the talking in meetings and within groups, along with the supervisor, manager, teacher, preacher, etc. The remaining ones made their way into their caves many years ago in school or in job experiences where this lesson was reinforced over and over again. The kid and many adults now think, "It's safe in here and I do not ever want to look stupid again."</u>

DISCUSSION: No one is the bad guy here. This is not about bad people. Not the teacher, who was never taught this leadership stuff. Not the kids (people), who laughed instinctively and never stopped. Not the dominators in team meetings you work with now. Not the ones who knew the answer(s).

Certainly the ones in the cave aren't bad people either although now they won't help with team decisions, problem solving, discussions, etc☺).

This is just a story to help you think about this LEARNING principle. How have you been impacted?"

<u>There are other societal factors and reasons that lead to this Non-LEARNER and Non-INVOLVEMENT mentality, but we'll save that for another day. For now just suffice it to say, there are many reasons that have led our society and people to not be *into* learning, but rather to do anything possible to avoid being the stupid one in group settings (so they remain quiet/in their cave).</u>

DISCUSSION: As we move forward in this principle of learning, please realize that you and many, many, many others have good reason for not being 'good' with talking in groups and with this learning principle. So digest the reasons for why you are where you are, and STARTING NOW, change your thinking of the value of learning and growing. How about this - when you don't know something, 1) you ask, 2) you learn, 3) now you know more than you did. What a concept, huh?!!!

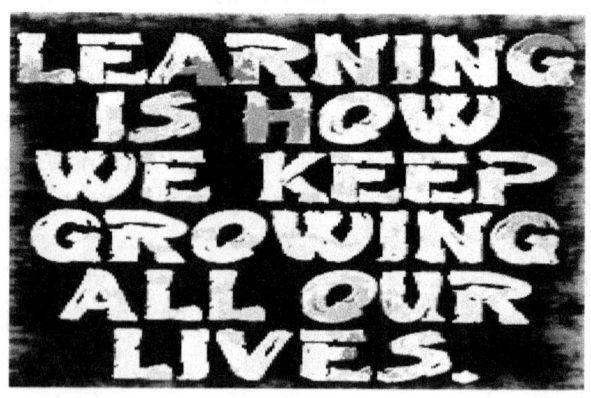

TALK #6 THINKING:

- **Takeaways**

- **Issues I need to think through and discuss with mentors**

- **What did Booker really intend here**

- **What do I want to add**

- **What are my concerns with this topic**

- **What might I need to discuss with my leader/boss?**

7

INDIVIDUAL VS TEAM

(WE ARE NOT GROWN TO BE TEAM THINKERS)

---

50 – 60 – 75?

...how effective is your team; or your organization's teams? Even if you say 75%, is this acceptable?

DISCUSSION: I want to talk to a dynamic I heard about recently, 'The impact of our INDIVIDUAL-focused Society'.

What makes developing and improving LEADERS, LEADERSHIP AND TEAMWORK such a big challenge for organizations?

Most everyone can spot an effective leader. We can understand what good leadership can do for a team, department or company. Who doesn't know what good teamwork is? Then why is IT so difficult to develop these dynamics within individuals, organizations and teams?

<u>Maybe brainstorm on the whiteboard some of their thoughts here before continuing?</u>

DISCUSSION: Maybe you don't see it as difficult? Take a moment and think about our organization. How many real leaders are here (and not just by their titles)? How is the organizational leadership and management? As you think of our department, team, section, division or other areas in our organization; how effective is the teamwork throughout?

Part of the answer to this challenge for organizations can be found by looking at our culture and society. Let me attempt to explain what I mean...

We are an *INDIVIDUALLY-focused* culture. From our first days in our youth and within the education mainstream, we focus on individual achievement. Think about this for a moment -- by the time an individual hits the work-world, where has leadership or teamwork been addressed? About the only real opportunity to learn the value of teamwork is through sports (or if you went through boot-camp in the military).

Unfortunately, even if we participated in sports, we are fortunate if we learned the right things about teamwork. This is dependent on the leadership (or lack of leadership) of the coach of that team. Regardless, many of us never participated in sports anyway. So where do we learn about leadership and teamwork?

Maybe you think about Boy/Girl Scouts or other type of youth programs; aren't they all pretty much about individual achievement? Isn't that all about earning the next badge or achieving the next individual level?

No wonder organizations struggle with these challenges. Nobody is doing anything wrong here you see; we have just learned too well – and not necessarily good or the right stuff. If we take this to the next logical argument, we find ourselves asking,

    Q: 'why don't we learn it once we get into the work-world by the organizations that employ us?'

    A: 'We hear teamwork preached, but then once again, people are recognized for their individual accomplishments. It is all just assumed and expected stuff within our culture; even though we were never taught it!

    What do we learn about how to move up that proverbial ladder? (And we are not even going to mention the politics argument here)! We learn to get up that ladder will come from developing a reputation for getting it done, ...being a self-starter, ...initiative, ...getting results, ...and the bottom line - succeeding no matter who/what gets in our way!!!

<u>I see it over and over in the management structure of organizations -- strong individual performers (and good people I might mention) rising up through the ranks.
But then the downfall for many of those people turns out to be closely tied to this thing called teamwork that they never really learned.
I think this might be closely associated to that long-known concept referred to as the Peter Principle... leave you to ponder that.</u>

DISCUSSION: Consider the enormous challenge for organizations in creating TEAMWORK:

- Leaders and Managers at the top who are not necessarily skilled at functioning on TEAMS (the management team they must now work with—other strong individual performers).

- Managers who are not necessarily very skilled at LEADING and BUILDING TEAMS; they know their stuff, just not the people-stuff.

- These leaders are expected to build teams with employees who also have been raised in this INDIVIDUAL-culture!

<u>You see, this model goes on over and over and over and over again.</u>

<u>This is the way it all works until there is a real commitment from the top in honestly looking at these issues through training, relationships & trust-building, openly communicating about practices, etc...</u>

<u>Don't look for that to happen anytime soon, which is why you are doing all this you realize!?!</u>

DISCUSSION: Another dynamic about our society's cultural impact on us is this: Even if I know and understand the need for coordination, teamwork, building relations, consulting others, being customer-focused, etc... our culture is about speed and producing NOW! This is all very contradictory; how do we deal with it gang?

<u>Consider how crazy this is - the next time we are in a brainstorming session, observe what happens when the group experiences a quiet pause!?! We tend to want to fill that pause instantaneously. We sure don't want to allow time for **thinking** to occur during brainstorming...do we now? YIKES</u>

TALK #7 THINKING:

- *Takeaways*

- *Issues I need to think through and discuss with mentors*

- *What did Booker really intend here*

- *What do I want to add*

- *What are my concerns with this topic*

- *What might I need to discuss with my leader/boss?*

8
NON-THREATENING ENVIRONMENT
(GETTING ALL ON THE TEAM)

> DEAR GOD
> IF I HURT OTHERS
> GIVE ME THE STRENGTH
> TO APOLOGIZE.
> IF PEOPLE HURT ME
> GIVE ME THE STRENGTH
> TO FORGIVE.
>
> *LASTLY IF I HAVE SOMEHOW
> HURT SOMEONE &
> DIDN'T REALIZE IT -
> HELP ME TO KNOW THIS (OR)
> SEND THEM TO ME SO
> I MAY FIX IT.
>
> ...relationships are everything!

DISCUSSION: Let's talk some more dynamics about TRUST. This will be a never ending topic for us and thinking I want us to always be conscientiously focused upon. Here's another aspect of it I want to dwell on a bit now:

KNOWINGLY LEADING!

Here is a question managers, teachers and leaders in general struggle with and discuss at times: *"How do you get people to speak up and talk in groups, team meetings, etc?"*

<u>*Like EVERYTHING in this book, use my words, thoughts, ideas and approaches in any way you wish (claim words, phrases or thoughts as yours, I don't care seriously).
I don't want you stewing about whose material this is, I want you to make this leadership thing work, have the conversations any way that works my friend!</u>

DISCUSSION: (A consultant friend shared these thoughts with me): Here are some keys to help you (us) with this thing called **T.R.U.S.T.**

___THREATENING environments often exist on teams

...you think not? Watch the next time you ask a group for input. Observe the dynamics of what occurs when people speak up and take the risk of being wrong, and subsequently being ridiculed, laughed at, etc.

<u>Consider the team you are on, with other managers, your peers ...that leadership team? Likely it is as bad as or worse than most teams regarding this dynamic (leader teams are typically worse than normal employee teams)!</u>

DISCUSSION: Levels of self-esteem are varied and the quiet ones are typically those that struggle with this and have been 'hurt' in the past when encouraged. This could have begun the first days of school (way back) when we are still excited and enthusiastic and eagerly want to be called upon.... After being laughed at (OR) not having your thought recognized (OR) told 'that won't work' -the mind and heart say "heck with this group stuff" for the rest of their lives!!!

   RELATIONSHIPS **must be right**...when you get serious about 'involvement, participation and team problem-solving', we must remember that this team has damaged relations, dominating people, etc. What has been the impact of new employees (who have been told they know nothing), etc? Past practices on our team must be addressed and informal rules put into place to create a new starting point. Rules are needed that encourage IMPROVED RELATIONS.

____**UNDERSTAND the impact we have on each other** ...the leader must make people realize how we tear each other down by our actions and words. Many of us have no intention to do so, but we can 'hurt' others and teamwork without even knowing it.

Q) Who gets to decide if what you said or did 'hurt'?
A) *The receiver* of course.
      Perception is reality—not what was meant, but what was perceived?!?

____**SEEK first to understand** ...'before seeking to be understood' is a phrase I borrowed that will do worlds of good for each of us if practiced. Once all of us team-members buy into this point – things will change and improve. In a nutshell, it means learn to let others speak first while you listen (sincerely) first. Consider the impact of you listening first—it says to the other person 'I value your opinion, thoughts and your side...' Once you have done this, most people will be more willing to listen (sincerely) to your side now!

TEAMS don't allow players to not-participate …the team must be part of making this work. You, the leader, will miss things and won't always be there. Place the responsibility on the team to 'police' each other, 'rat' on each other and generally correct each other as we grow, develop and improve as a team.

<u>TRUST has so many deep meanings and realizations for us as leaders. I hope that this has helped a little.</u>

DISCUSSION: Allow me to make one other last point: people will tell you that this stuff is no big deal. TRUST me, *it is*…I know it and so do YOU! Commit to addressing the keys above and we will be overwhelmed with input and maybe I will be left asking "how do I control people, all the talking, input and too many ideas"??!

<u>Maybe something to share here?</u>

KNOWINGLY LEADING!

Please don't toss this aside too quickly...wait for a quiet moment, read & consider the implications for you and your organization's culture—and YOUR TEAM!...

(...by the way, the essence of the content here is from something I used to have hanging on the wall in my home, but don't have anymore, nor do I know who to credit with the content.)

EVERYTHING LEADERS (AND ALL OF US) NEED TO KNOW

IF >We Live with Criticism...We Learn to Condemn.

IF >We Live with Hostility...We Learn to Fight.

IF >We Live with Ridicule...We Learn to be Shy.

IF >We Live with Shame...We Learn to feel Guilty.

IF >We Live with Tolerance...We Learn to be Patient.

IF >We Live with Praise...We Learn to Appreciate.

IF >We Live with Fairness...We Learn Justice.

IF >We Live with Approval...We Learn to Like Ourselves.

IF >We Live with Acceptance and Friendship...

...We find the World (and workplace) to be
Good and Positive!...

What is our organization living & practicing?

TALK #8 THINKING:

❖ *Takeaways*

❖ *Issues I need to think through and discuss with mentors*

❖ *What did Booker really intend here*

❖ *What do I want to add*

❖ *What are my concerns with this topic*

❖ *What might I need to discuss with my leader/boss?*

9
THOSE 'OTHERS'

(UNDERSTANDING WE ALL NEED IN EACH OTHER)

I have come to believe that the key to:

Success ···Peace ···Happiness ···Significance & Leadership

Is a MIND & HEART that is

FOCUSED ON OTHERS

DISCUSSION: A funny, interesting and very real dynamic I heard a while back; as we continue to focus more on us and this (our) team…

Specifically, the point I'm referring to is about the challenge of leading and working with others; not ALL others – just those few that make it difficult. You know the ones I'm referring to – those OTHERS in our lives.

We all have those people that we effectively relate to, like, trust, enjoy, happy to be around, communicate with well, etc? AND, don't we also have those OTHERS, that don't quite live up to

our expectations or just can't do enough 'good things' to make us like them? You know the ones we tell others about... ☺
Of course we do, so what's the answer? What is needed here for any highly successful team or even any relationship between two people is unconditional acceptance of one another! I fear that this is easier said than done, huh? The more likely handling of these people is one of," I need you to prove yourself". It becomes a trap we all fall into as we attempt to work with others; we might call this trap 'performance-based acceptance'. In other words, our acceptance of each other is tied to our ability to live up to each other's expectations of others.

<u>Here's a biblical reference: interesting how 'we cannot do enough good works' to earn our salvation or to receive His Grace.</u>

<u>However among us humans, we are totally about 'what you can do to earn/keep our relationship'.</u>

DISCUSSION: You see though, this is nearly impossible, maybe based on the fact that we are all so different from one another. So 'performance-based acceptance' becomes a trap in the sense that we are all not the same in our thoughts, actions, habits, ethics, etc. So we struggle, fight or just avoid each other - when you are an OTHER to me.

The only solution is hard, persistent work between people on RELATIONSHIP or maybe, maintain an agreement to unconditional acceptance. We need accountabilities in place - to agree to alert each other of when we 'do things' that tug at this acceptance (relationship). This is not to mean that we should not have expectations of each other; or be accountable to each other.

Here's a scenario for us to think through:

So here we are, Bob and I talking about the 8 employees that he supervises…and he says "Well, 6 of the 8 are just fine, it's just those other two!" Or same sort of deal, different scenario… 'Sitting there talking with Ruth about her co-workers'.

<u>Important point: I need you to realize that these co-workers could be a team at the top-level of management, exec-level, in a front-office, out in the shop, within our cubicles or wherever. It happens anywhere and everywhere.</u>

DISCUSSION: Anyway, Ruth is telling me about how well she works with most of the people in her department, "it's just ol' so-and-so, he's just hopeless!"

<u>LEADERSHIP PERSPECTIVE: Now the insinuation here from these fictitious characters is that the majority of the people are good due to my fine leadership or my abilities to relate to others.</u>

<u>Note that they didn't necessarily say these words, but they were implied in the discussion.</u>

DISCUSSION: Leaders think this stuff about their Leader/Follower relations, "Most of the people are good, because of my leadership, hard work and effectiveness in working with them?"

But not so quick -- let me offer another perspective - which I always try to tactfully relate to people in these discussions. For most of us, we might want to assume that the majority of the folks we work with are the result of my superb leadership or people-skills...maybe. Maybe not. Then again 'that majority' that we lead &/or work with might just be the ones that we naturally can work with because of compatibility. For whatever reason though, the majority are the easy ones.

KNOWINGLY LEADING!

<u>*This is all very connected to the BAD APPLE concept discussed in Chapter 23.</u>

DISCUSSION: Now comes the tough part for us, as leaders or as team-members…dealing with the 'others'.

Whether we are a leader or an employee/co-worker; here is where our **leadership and relationship-building skills** are really needed, challenged, tested…AND oftentimes missing! Instead, of doing the hard work and applying our superb relationship-skills, we just write those people off as hopeless …as OTHERS.

<u>BUT IN FACT, THOSE 'OTHERS' ARE THE ONES THAT REALLY CHALLENGE AND TEST US…AND ULTIMATELY DEMONSTRATE OUR SKILLS/TALENTS IN LEADERSHIP, RELATIONSHIP-BUILDING AND BUILDING TEAMS!!!</u>

DISCUSSION: How hard we try, how much success we have with 'others' will likely have a lasting impact on your success in the workplace. Want to move up...want to move on? Want a raise? Develop these skills! This is a message for you, me, all of us sitting here; something I want us to BE!

Our leaders are watching and our success in relationships will likely play a big role in where you (and I) go from here.... This applies to all of us.

Don't agree? Let's discuss....

TALK #9 THINKING:

- ❖ **Takeaways**

- ❖ **Issues I need to think through and discuss with mentors**

- ❖ **What did Booker really intend here**

- ❖ **What do I want to add**

- ❖ **What are my concerns with this topic**

- ❖ **What might I need to discuss with my leader/boss?**

10

BOTTLENECKS

(EVERY TEAM HAS THEM)

> SURROUND YOURSELF WITH PEOPLE WHO MAKE YOU A BETTER PERSON

DISCUSSION: An interesting thought hit me the other day...

On my way to wherever I was going (?), I was pondering teamwork and more specifically *this* team; and something hit me that I want to share with you.

It struck me that both - teams and organizational operational systems - deal with what in the manufacturing world is known as 'bottlenecks'.

So we're on common ground, let me offer this definition of a bottleneck:

> *'...a point within a process/system where the flow and/or productivity is slowed down and where extra effort, attention or resources must be expended to address the problem. You won't find that in Webster's—but it will suffice to get us on the same page...'*
>
> [paraphrased from various sources].

Now here's what struck me as a new perspective regarding teamwork. Consider this for a moment – TEAMS are much like any operation, system or process – think of it as your/our PEOPLE-SYSTEM.

With both, it is a matter of everything being in sync; but instead of machinery, parts, mechanics and hardware, we are speaking of working relationships, roles and expectations understood, etc. Each operation or piece of machinery (or person) must support the other parts/pieces (people) for teamwork to flow. When people function well together, the result is a highly efficient and productive process in terms of meeting goals and objectives. That's that *great team* we all have heard about huh? It's about us as we have visioned us to be - going from a 7.0 to a 10!

That is precisely what team-building is all about, isn't it? It is Continuous Improvement of our PEOPLE SYSTEM.

<u>Message to Leaders? ...understand and realize the impact of bottlenecks on the team's productivity and ultimate success. It's not just what you should understand and deal with - IT'S YOUR JOB!</u>

DISCUSSION: Let's toss around the challenge of identifying, improving and eliminating bottlenecks. All teams have bottlenecks - and it is not productive to be sitting there right now thinking of Bob, Sue, or someone else that you probably view as a problem. You see, then that makes YOU a bottlenecking dynamic! ☺ Ponder that for a moment...

We don't address it (Bottlenecks of our People-System) by laying blame on other players individually...no we ID the issue and work on it systemically.

The bottom line is that we all take turns at one time or another, being a bottleneck in people-systems and these have an impact on the overall success (pace, productivity, quality, etc) of the TEAM. Here are some of the bottlenecks that come to mind; think of these and see if you come up with others:

- **CAPABILITY** (knowledge, know-how, education, training and experience to do the job).

- **RELATIONSHIPS** (open-ness, transparency, understanding and acceptance of others).

- **NEW PLAYERS** (new people to the team can't become productive and effective on the team until accepted, comfortable, competent, trusted and relations established; and the newness fear is overcome).

- **PAST ISSUES** (unresolved conflict, issues or problems that individuals have had with others on the team. Typically these are carried around as baggage or grudges or minimally, being uncooperative with others).

- **ATTITUDES / NEGATIVISM** (some of us don't realize how important this overly used word is; as I carry around my attitude on my coat-sleeve...others see it and avoid us. That hurts us, the team).

- **COMMUNICATION** (when I fail to communicate openly and effectively with other team members, it affects the overall team's efficiency. This can be intentional, un-realized or purely accidental).

- **UNCLEAR ROLES / EXPECTATIONS** (can be a failure of the organization or leaders to clarify functional areas OR that a team member sees his/her role one way and others see it another way. Conflict, misunderstanding and unfairness *thoughts* settle in and begin to raise their ugly head).

- **PERSONALITY – DIFFERENCES / DIVERSITY** (it's reality—it needs to be understood, studied, overcome and utilized to our advantage).

- **UNRESOLVED CONFLICTS / MISUNDERSTANDINGS** (someone did or said something that you took the wrong way and you decide to hold it against them for the rest of their lives. That's insanity and such a waste).

- **TRUST** (a team cannot reach peak performance and success without it. We gotta have trust in each other to do our part, fulfill commitments, meet deadlines, raise issues, identify bottlenecks, respect feelings, opinions and thoughts).

- **OTHERS**...................

Message to Team-members? (which we all are): Take responsibility to help other members of the team / peers see and overcome their bottleneck…or yours!

KNOWINGLY LEADING!

DISCUSSION: It's not just the leader's job! The sooner we deal with them - the sooner we become a well-oiled machine, operation, system, and 'TEAM'.

Last but not least, when we do *nothing* about these situations, but just allow them to exist day after day after day, then we are practicing 'insanity'.

<u>...write on board prior maybe?</u>

DISCUSSION: Allowing bottlenecks to exist unresolved; this might be defined by some as:

"DOING THE SAME THING OVER AND OVER AND OVER, AND EXPECTING DIFFERENT RESULTS"

...think about it.

<u>The following is a GREAT exercise, concept and challenge I pose to teams all the time. Strongly recommend you talk to it and then set up an accountability aspect to this to 'make it happen' within the players on your team. Tie to the bottlenecking concept for sure.</u>

DISCUSSION: "OK, so let's talk TEAM. How are we; we improving?

Let's connect to our vision, the culture we want, LEADERSHIP QUALITIES, etc. What is the impact of a bad relationship, conflicts on the team, etc?

So here's my challenge and an accountability I am putting on all of us; consider these questions.

    Q: Who is the worst relationship (bottleneck) you have with someone on the team? Is it possible that poor relationship could NOT be affecting the team?
    A: ….of course not, it has to be impacting productivity, flow, etc.

Now think about this, but don't say anything out loud. I want you to focus on who that worst relationship is that you have with someone on this team right here? Who is your worst relationship on our team? Everyone has a 'worst'…

What would it mean if everyone, all of us to include me, fixed their worst relationship?

What would that mean to our current rating of our team (that we did earlier)? _____ (7.0?) If all those relationships were improved, what would it do to this number?

By this time next month, I want each of us to go fix your/our worst relationship. We will discuss collectively and also in your 1:1 monthly evaluation; this IS an expectation I am adding to your job description!

TALK #10 THINKING:

- ❖ **Takeaways**

- ❖ **Issues I need to think through and discuss with mentors**

- ❖ **What did Booker really intend here**

- ❖ **What do I want to add**

- ❖ **What are my concerns with this topic**

- ❖ **What might I need to discuss with my leader/boss?**

There's always
a little truth behind every
"just kidding,"
a little knowledge behind every
"I don't know,"
a little emotion behind every
"I don't care,"
and a little pain behind every
"It's okay."

11

NEWBIES MISS OUT ON ALL THIS!

(CULTURAL DEVELOPMENT DEPENDS ON IT)

365

....the number of days per year leaders need to be conscious of all the 'stuff' in these conversations; leading to a culture continually improving.

<u>This is not so much of a lengthy conversation to have with your team, but rather a tip here for you as a leader. I would recommend you involving them in this dynamic on some level periodically.</u>

<u>Think about all these previous conversations (and the ones that follow) from this book, and their intent. Now think about how you bring on (hire) new people onto the team. Is there a 'real' orientation process: and is there, a process where you bring new leaders up to speed with all these conversations?</u>

<u>The typical manager just wings this stuff; the typical newbie doesn't get this stuff! (Except accidentally and incidentally over time). What's the cost?</u>

<u>Of course he/she (the leader/YOU) speaks to the newbie as we welcome them *in some way* onto the team; but how do they know all this stuff that you have been doing (conversations) with the team all along?</u>

<u>Brainstorm this with your team, to help YOU make sure your LEADER'S NEWBIE CHECKLIST is a good one?</u>

<u>Betting you don't even have a NEWBIE CHECKLIST, hummmmmm. Recommend you have one for employees in general and one specifically for your subordinate leaders hired.</u>

<u>***This is not about any HR Orientation procedure in place.</u>

DISCUSSION: I need your help in creating (and/or updating) my checklist I use when we bring new people onto the team. Consider all we are, what we have become, what our values, practices and principles are; …what goes on that checklist?

What are the things you want to make sure a new co-worker/peer knows about 'how we do things here'?

KNOWINGLY LEADING!

Every leader should create and continually develop a file/document with items to discuss with new people. Otherwise necessary things don't get said, cultures do not remain consistent and all the newbie has to go on is *his/her past cultures, potentially bad previous models, own misconceptions* of behavior, etc.

REAL LEADERS don't leave this to chance (or just wing these initial discussions).

***This is a quick sample that I would include if I were the leader; what's yours look like? If I can help you develop yours further, feel free to buzz me.

LEADERS MASTER CHECKLIST FOR NEW TEAM MEMBERS:

- Our culture here

- Growing you to be me (my up-line position)

- Growing your people/team to be you

- Our monthly conversations – YOU now, YOU future, YOUR people now/future

- Leader Quality talk…OUR Leader & team competencies

- Resources for growing you (me, mentors, coaches, peers,

subordinates)

- Don't surprise me with 'the system was broke'
- Monthly talks will be about YOU and me; no operations - numbers – technical job function stuff
- Vision the perfect me, …and you
- Vision the perfect team
- Praise in Public, Reprimand in Private
- ETA
- Teaching Fishing
- Cultures, here and where you have been
- Leaders don't stop when problems exist, knock down barriers to include me
- Open Door
- Loyalty to the Absent, Rumor, gossip,
- Smoking, other behavior habit issues
- My quirks and absolutes …and yours?!?
- Organizational relationships to fix, maintain, nurture
- I don't assume anything about us, your leadership prep, etc
- Freedom to Fail, Risk-taking

- ➤ Principles and Practices of mine…?

- ➤ Attitude of workforce about hiring from within?

- ➤ Organization's current/past evaluation and assessing people

- ➤ What is your belief about developing your subordinates?

- ➤ Relationships with senior management in our organization?

- ➤ Your expectations, concerns and maybe personal issues I need to know…

- ➤ Love to know you and your family better…

<u>*NOTE: In case it's not obvious by now, every conversation/chapter within this book should be on this list. Maybe a copy of the book handed out!</u>

TALK #11 THINKING:

- ❖ **Takeaways**

- ❖ **Issues I need to think through and discuss with mentors**

- ❖ **What did Booker really intend here**

- ❖ **What do I want to add**

- ❖ **What are my concerns with this topic**

- ❖ **What might I need to discuss with my leader/boss?**

12

WHO ARE YOU?

(THEY NEED TO KNOW YOU)

The Principles & Practices of
SIGNIFICANCE

- Peace
- Transparent
- Forgiving
- Love / Relationship
- Learner
- Service
- Thankful
- Fruitful

"How we live our life matters!"

DISCUSSION: I want to talk to you about VALUES and PRINCIPLES; yours, mine and ours.

MY SIGNIFICANCE Principles. Our company here has Core Values, I want you to know mine…………

<u>The point here is to suggest all leaders should have a set of principles, values, etc. I am presenting these from a book of mine called, 'SIGNIFICANCE Starts Now')</u>

<u>My principles are here to prompt you to do some thinking on this and develop and intertwine YOURS into your culture, leader qualities and vision talks. All these should mesh together and clarify where we are going collectively, individually – our People System.</u>

DISCUSSION: We should have direction, a compass, principles and values we want 'us to be'. All these should have some connectivity to our vision we created, that earlier conversation. They should also have application and connectivity to my Leadership Qualities/Competencies you all said you wanted in me. Let me attempt to explain and connect....

<u>Replace these with yours?</u>

1. PEACE...

2. THANKFUL...

3. SERVICE...

4. FORGIVENESS...

5. LEARNING…

6. LOVE & RELATIONSHIP…

7. TRANSPARENCY…

8. FRUITFUL…

Again, these eight are mine to make a point. This is about YOU and your leadership and management approach. Many leaders will never go into this kind of depth about themselves; I would. Your choice.
If you have any interest in my book mentioned here or maybe just want to read, ponder and think about the principles of mine above – here is link to the book:
'SIGNIFICANCE Starts Now – How We Live Our Life Matters' (click here or copy/paste this link into your browser - http://goo.gl/CChCNv

DISCUSSION: Additionally, I want to speak just a bit more to who I am, your leader and what you should expect of me and know about what's important to me.

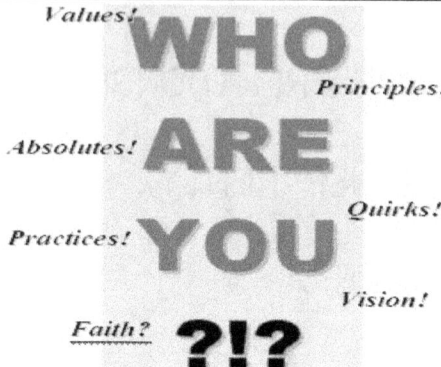

- ✓ What are my QUIRKS...?
- ✓ What are my NON-NEGOTIABLES...?
- ✓ What are my ABSOLUTES...?
- ✓ Who am I? Pet peeves, weirdisms, how I am wired, etc. Who are you?

<u>I believe all these have application into workplace / organizational value systems. That's just me however.</u>

<u>What are yours? Do you see this as a conversation? The quicker and more transparent the leader – the quicker and</u>

KNOWINGLY LEADING!

more productive are relationships, teamwork and well ....success.

A lack of transparency is in itself a Bottleneck huh?

DISCUSSION: What are yours? Let's take some time to see if ALL of this, the company values, mine, yours, the teams, etc – are all synched?

An example to demonstrate all this (feel free to adapt and use as your story☺):

Years ago, (actually during my time in military), two new officers arrived at the unit. Making this brief – the Commander brought us in to just do a quick initial orientation. One thing he told us that has always stuck with me as a leader; he told this about himself.

'I know I walk around with this scowl on my face and that serious look makes people believe I am mad, etc. Not the case, it is just what I tend to do and because I am always thinking, I come off that way. I have come to realize I must tell people this on the front end, so it doesn't impact our relationship.' He turned out to be one of the greatest friends I ever had and a super leader. He was right, he did scowl. It was so smart of him to share this with people.

Lessons... **?**

TALK #12 THINKING:

- ❖ *Takeaways*

- ❖ *Issues I need to think through and discuss with mentors*

- ❖ *What did Booker really intend here*

- ❖ *What do I want to add*

- ❖ *What are my concerns with this topic*

- ❖ *What might I need to discuss with my leader/boss?*

13

TRUST KILLERS

(CONVERSATIONS CAN NEVER END)

These are all different dynamics that play out in many organizations and corporate America related to cultural TRUST.

Strongly recommend you study these, apply them to your workplace, talk to these and seek others (TRUST-BREAKERS) from the team?

DISCUSSION:

Workload and Scheduling: "We won't be working Saturday; ...or we won't be working late tonight" ...common ploy of leaders to keep people motivated until later in the day/week when we drop the surprise bomb on them and work after all. That's motivating all right; like they don't view this as being lied to..."

Make sure I don't do anything like this; I hope to be clear and direct in our relationship. Thoughts...?

Quality First: This is a BIGGEE... companies preach this, print it on 'Values' cards to carry around, put it on walls and then tell people to shut up and 'ship it' after they identify a problem, flaw, etc.

What are we doing that contradicts our values here ...anything?

KNOWINGLY LEADING!

TEAMWORK – (Teams Solve Problems, Not Individuals)

Time after time, we (management) make decisions and provide solutions for them to execute. We (management) seem to suggest, 'just trust us, this is the best thing since sliced bread and expect full-fledged buy-in. We never consulted with *them*, asked their opinions or attempted to gain buy-in.

[Then management wonders: "What could be causing them to be so upset?"]

> # THERE'S NO
> # I
> # IN TEAM
> *... unless of course the* **I** *is management, the manager!*

***This dynamic is spoken to more in-depth in the chapter on CHANGE.

DISCUSSION: Tell us When You See a Problem: We ask for the truth, but when people deliver the bad news or criticism we (management) don't like to hear - we blow them away. Maybe we are 'shooting the messenger' ...which, by the way, is a great way to prevent messages from getting to you (management) in the future! Think about this...

We (I) do anything like this to you guys?

Suggestion boxes must go! Not many things send all the wrong signals more than having a Suggestion Box on the wall. This is one of my pet peeves as a leader. Think about what it says when we ask people to put their ideas on a little piece of paper and stick it in that box? It says, we recognize you cannot talk to your leader/chain of command; we'll get around to you if we have time; we realize you feel the need to be anonymous, etc....

SUGGESTION BOX
(Because we want to hear your suggestions
Even though your leader doesn't?!?)

I want anything and everything you want/need to communicate, to come straight to me. The relationship I am building with all of us, with each of you is for that reason. Thoughts?

We want Risk-Takers! Time after time we abuse, ridicule, or in other ways, put down people for having taken risks. Risk is OK as long as it doesn't fail or cause us any problems, right?!?

Promotions, Raises, Transfers... How many times do you think that someone in your organization has considered himself or herself to be the right person for the job, only to have given it to someone else?

<u>*How to do EVALUATION, FEEDBACK & ASSESSMENT is discussed in Chapter 14.</u>

DISCUSSION: When we don't have a system for evaluating performance, people will consider our system unfair... and it probably is! We are building an environment of 'it's not what you know, but who you know!" And we (management) will have a tough time proving them wrong!

This won't be us here on this team, we are going to do feedback right – hopefully you are already seeing this in how we do things on this team?

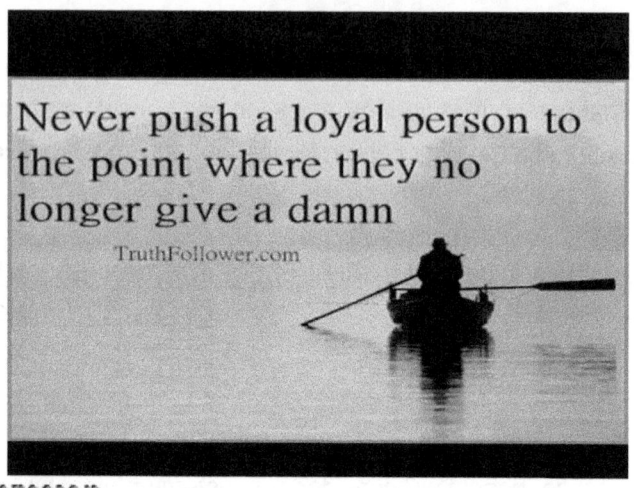

DISCUSSION: Let me check on it, and I'll get back to you.

Take a moment and think how many times we have heard this said to people and someone failed 'to get back to us.' I'm not suggesting that someone intentionally lied, but isn't it the same thing to that person?

I realize I am likely going to forget, so here's how I am going to outsmart myself; I need your help with this. I am giving you the right to pester me until I get back to you. Let me clarify...

<u>This is a concept called TAKING MONKEYS ON YOUR BACK, which many in leadership roles do un-knowingly with all the best of intentions.</u>

<u>Ponder all this and teach it/share with them....</u>

KNOWINGLY LEADING!

DISCUSSION: I heard this leadership-issue many years ago and want to share it with you to make sure I don't do this with you. It is an issue related TRUST, DELEGATION, ACCOUNTABILITY and LEADERSHIP. Briefly it is about an awareness all leaders need as we wander around the workplace (this is also great learning for any/all of us as we wander through our lives with others, at work, play, home, family, etc).

For leaders specifically, they move throughout their day's work 'taking on monkeys' without realizing it.

> Every time you feel yourself getting pulled into other people's nonsense, repeat these words:
>
> **NOT MY CIRCUS,**
>
> **NOT MY MONKEYS.**
>
> ((POLISH PROVERB))

Picture this: the manager wanders around through the workday and people bring issues, problems and questions to him/her. In seemingly doing the right thing, the manager says "let me check it out and get back to you".

<u>*This concept has connection to TEACHING FISHING (Chapter 4); I will leave it to you to do the connecting.</u>

DISCUSSION: Q: What has just happened?   A: The manager just took the MONKEY on his/her back.

The issue is now his/hers - the manager's! The manager continues onward thru the day 'taking on other monkeys'.

The manager is setting himself up to *break trust* as he *unintentionally* forgets about this monkey – leaving the person waiting to hear back…..
The person who gave you (the wandering leader) the monkey is left with thoughts such as...

"YOU DON'T CARE; I KNEW SHE WOULD DO NOTHING ABOUT THIS; YOU CANNOT TRUST HIM TO DO ANYTHING FOR YOU; HE LET ME DOWN AGAIN; MY BOSS IS USELESS, LIAR…….."

How many monkeys are you (the manager, parent, teacher, friend, teacher, etc.) carrying around on your back and don't even know it? This happens between any two people as well; is it possible you are carrying around monkeys you have taken from one of your co-workers here?

KNOWINGLY LEADING!

SOLUTION:
Q: First realize who this problem is important to..?
A: The one who gave it to you, right?

I intend to start using a different approach: Keep the monkey on *your* back. Change my words to this "Let me check it out and get back to you. However because I may get overwhelmed with other monkeys, if you don't hear back by this Friday, remind (pester, dog, harass) me about it"

Get it …make sense?

TALK #13 THINKING:

❖ **Takeaways**

❖ **Issues I need to think through and discuss with mentors**

❖ **What did Booker really intend here**

❖ **What do I want to add**

❖ **What are my concerns with this topic**

❖ **What might I need to discuss with my leader/boss?**

14

EVALUATION & FEEDBACK

(WE NEED EACH OTHER)

Performance Assessment, Evaluation, Feedback, Critiquing, etc...

These are concepts critical to the workplace, individuals, on teams and to the leader. Most people have had them executed VERY poorly and ineffectively in their past (I imagine you have as well). Of course many of those you now lead, may possibly have literally NEVER seen anything done in these regards.

We must change the mindset of people; with each individual and

<u>maybe within yourself – about Performance Assessment, Evaluation, Feedback, Critiquing, etc</u>
<u>There is much here to digest; take your time, consider what's here. Develop/design your process and go make it happen...</u>

DISCUSSION: '...We ALL need help!' It's hard to argue with that, huh?

<u>I realized something a few years back while in transition, looking & searching for so many things - to include a job☺!</u>

<u>In conversations with a new friend/business acquaintance, this dynamic of 'seeking & accepting input from others' became such a good lesson for me. Boy did I need some help.</u>

<u>The bottom line here? We all need input, assistance, mentors and coaches in our lives—ALL of us.</u>

DISCUSSION: I want to share some thinking here regarding 'first impressions'; as well as the value of feedback and input.

This was shared with me by a close friend and now Exec Coach I now utilize from time to time. His story:

"....Because of very dramatic changes in my life, I had become conscious / concerned of a void that had resulted – not having people around to give me honest input, coaching and thoughts about ME. Now, because of the world of leadership and training that I live in, this dynamic is something that I believe in & point out to those with whom I work.

Quite by chance I stumbled into the path of someone who helped fill that void for me. It took some boldness on his part, but I received invaluable input, observations and critiquing of ME. Some bad habits & behaviors had developed and needed addressing in marketing myself.

As I was receiving this input, I had the choice to make – "Do I get mad at 'these things' I was hearing about ME? Was I going to reject the input or thank this person for their input…?"

<u>Consider what's significant of this story to use in your teaching?</u>

DISCUSSION: By the way, how do (we) respond to input, critiquing, etc? For many people, hearing negatives about themselves typically ruins their day huh? How about you?

Our response to input and critique should be, as Gomer Pyle used to say (and maybe still does☺)… "THANK YOU, THANK YOU, THANK YOU!"

Why? …because this person has just HELPED you!

<u>For me, these observations back then were spot on – just a few little quirks, jargon picked up, appearance issues, etc. These were habits I had developed unconsciously.</u>

DISCUSSION: I thought about how many people may have written me off or thought less of me because of those quirks (those initial impressions)? Why didn't THEY tell me right then and there?

You and I know the answer. They didn't feel comfortable enough; the relationship wasn't strong enough or they didn't want to hurt my feelings, right? What's the message here?

<u>You and I must have those people in our lives to help us, to point out the flaws we do not see. If you have no one like this, find someone! Seek out a mentor(s) who can help you before you go do one more interview, hit another networking event or find yourself around other people you want to impress.</u>

DISCUSSION: Do you really want to know the answer when you ask people their opinion?

Don't ask others if you don't want to hear the bad news. Please do realize that those who offer nothing for you to work on are useless to you – think about that! It might be worth considering about those in our lives we call friends – are they adding value to you!?! It kinda gets into that management dynamic about leaders hiring 'YES MEN'.

KNOWINGLY LEADING!

We must learn to value other input besides our own opinions, thoughts and beliefs. After all you (and I, all of us) are a bit biased when it comes to ourselves! And two heads are always better than one!

<u>Consider how you transition to establishing competencies for you to use in growing ourselves (you, the team, etc). Obviously this ties to the LEADER QUALITIES chapter/conversation here. That talk should go prior to this one?</u>

DISCUSSION: We need competencies to use in growing our selves. These are about you, me, the team overall; and will be used from day one when someone joins our team as well. These must tie to the culture and that vision we all decided upon earlier. Here is just a sample I created from our list and I want us to discuss and agree upon something to begin with; this can evolve and *should* evolve over time.

<u>I realize you are possibly creating something here ...when there is something already available likely through HR/the organization's admin. You must tie all this together; holler if I can help you think through this...</u>

Realize also that LEADER competencies and EMPLOYEE competencies and qualities are likely very similar. Study on this. Again this is not here (below) to be the right or perfect list; just a thought-starter.

KNOWINGLY LEADING!

LEADERSHIP PERFORMANCE COMPETENCIES

Rate each area from 10 to 1, comments at bottom or on back of form (10: high / best -- 1: worst / poor)

1. **BUSINESS/JOB KNOWLEDGE** ____
   education, self-development, development of others, operational/technical competence, learner,

2. **COMMUNICATIONS** ____
   counseling, listening, people informed, written, expectations, presentation, teaching, evaluation, inspire

3. **PROBLEM SOLVING / DECISION MAKING** ____
   judgment, conflict resolution, consensus, involving, reasoning, delegation, thinking, selling / convincing

4. **RELATIONSHIPS** ____
   caring, respect, fairness, understanding, supporting, loyalty, compassion, cross-functions, teamwork, peers, external

5. **PROCESS IMPROVEMENT** ____
   empowering, continuous improvement, open-minded, adaptive / flexible, systems-thinking, safety, change

6. **INFLUENCE** ____
   teaching, inspiring, charisma, growing people & teams, influence, involves people, cooperation,

7. **PRODUCTIVITY/RESULTS** ____
   making it happen, endurance, mission accomplishment, attainment of goals, deadlines...

8. **PLANNING & ORGANIZING** ____
   time management, planning, reliability, visioning, structured, expectations, deadlines, controls,

9. **PROFESSIONALISM** ____
   appearance, accountable, presence, attitude, standards, example, sensitivity, policy, courage,

10. **ETHICS/TRUST** ____
    work ethic, honest, values, culture, integrity, fairness, takes ownership, loyalty to the absent, dependable

DISCUSSION: We are going to begin a REAL process that looks like this...

<u>*Talk to this with a calendar-year approach to simplify understanding.</u>

DISCUSSION:

- ✓ Long-term stuff...Real change is not some short-term program, magic pill, or get-away/retreat for the gang or some one-time workshop.

- ✓ It is never-ending feedback & accountabilities tied to that feedback.

- ✓ The Leader buying-in regarding how we change behavior and then leading the way intentionally.

- ✓ Creating a mindset of Feedback/Critique/Evaluation being a 'positive vs a negative'.

- ✓ Real behavioral change happening only thru real targeted assessment & conversation; followed by specific coaching and training in those identified areas of weakness...

***<u>I avoid trying to tell an organization or leader what they need in terms of 'Leadership Skills Training' - until the organizational leadership sets a target (competencies) & then through evaluation identifies Real needs that the leader understands he/she needs.</u>

DISCUSSION:

- ✓ We begin making evaluation 'real' and not inflated.... We break the practice of everyone being a 9 or 10.

- ✓ It is about commitment to developing our most valuable resource – PEOPLE, and LEADERS!

Here is a Process (STEPS) I want us to explore:

- Form or tool (the one above or one you create with them) provided to employee.

- Employee evaluates self and returns to Leader (prior to actual scheduled monthly meeting).

- Leader/Employee sit down and discuss differences and essentially do a gap-analysis. This is talking through the differences of how the employee sees things and how the leader sees things.

<u>This can be squirmy and uncomfortable the first few times. The leader needs to stay real and reinforce this is a monthly dialogue/process and the goal is continuous improvement. It is about 'improving' along with a focus on year end.</u>

DISCUSSION:

- This conversation between leader/follower takes place every month; follower accountable to get on leader's calendar and send updated evaluation of self to leader (few days prior).

- Each monthly talk stresses the point, 'this is how I see you if were next December/end of the year, final evaluation time. Softens the blow, because we have the rest of the year to improve…

- Emphasis again is always placed on growing ourselves, continuous improvement and doing things better; so end of year formal assessment is:

KNOWINGLY LEADING!

- ❖ Fair
- ❖ Non-surprising
- ❖ Accurate
- ❖ Real
- ❖ …and everyone doesn't get the same 'grade' because you did it right this time…

EVALUATE NOW, …not in December!

I recommend a strong thorough study by the leader on how to do all this well.

There is always a tendency to talk just the operationally, technical, job-function stuff; avoiding the tough stuff such as: (team-player, relations, behaviors, habits, motivation, attitude, supportiveness, professionalism, etc)

ANOTHER SUGGESTION: It may be a good idea to approach this challenge by having two meetings / month:

1) One on ONLY how well they do the job hired for and

2) Second meeting ONLY to be on the other stuff; the hard stuff, typically avoided (no talking about the operational stuff).

TALK #14 THINKING:

- ❖ *Takeaways*

- ❖ *Issues I need to think through and discuss with mentors*

- ❖ *What did Booker really intend here*

- ❖ *What do I want to add*

- ❖ *What are my concerns with this topic*

- ❖ *What might I need to discuss with my leader/boss?*

15

THE FAMILY IMPACT

(WHERE WE CAME FROM, WHAT WE LEARNED)

> **TREAT EMPLOYEES LIKE THEY MAKE A DIFFERENCE AND THEY WILL.**
> — Jim Goodnight, CEO, SAS

<u>**My Assumption #1.**</u> <u>An abundance of people in every organization, at all levels, stress over the ineffectiveness of our boss as well as poor relationships with co-workers. These two dynamics (ineffective Leadership and Teamwork) consume an enormous amount of wasted, non-productive time – bottlenecks! Obviously this time 'could' be spent producing your product or providing your service, and oh by the way making more profits. RIGHT? Wasted time = Lost dollars.</u>

DISCUSSION:

Your Organization's Unconscious Assumption #1. People are hired into organizations with well-developed skill sets of: interpersonal communications, working through conflict, playing well with others, relationship-building, teamwork understanding, respecting others, honesty, listening skills, trustworthiness and honesty...

This is true because we all come from solid backgrounds (families, previous models, school, society in general), where we have seen and practiced these traits/skills.

WRONG! Fact: Increasingly, people are coming from family and lifetimes of dysfunction (work, home, play). People do not show up with interpersonal, team skills, etc.

Your Organization's Unconscious Assumption #2. Anyone can lead people - once they have put in the time and developed the knowledge base about the product we produce/service we provide.

WRONG! Fact: How has that been working for you...and how did leaders really get there? Seniority and experience are the norm reasoning; and I won't even mention that sometimes becoming a manager/supervisor is about politics or education.

Your Organization's Unconscious Assumption #3. We can bring in some outside consultant/trainer to do TEAMBUILDING workshops or do SUPERVISOR training (if/when we ever have any excess $ in the budget), and that will solve the incorrectness of Assumptions 1 and 2.

WRONG! Fact: We are pumped for a bit, but then tomorrow my same screwed-up boss or co-worker will be there. Typically no behavioral change occurs; no accountabilities put into place to change anything back at the ranch (after the training or workshop)

<u>**My Assumption #2.** Because of these organizational/societal assumptions, ALL organizations are performing somewhere between 60-75% of what their potential is. I realize this suggests only the 'best of the best' companies out there are performing at only 75%! I believe this to be true.</u>

My Assumption #3. Your organization (or team) and all others have become numb to these assumptions. They have unconsciously accepted them (these assumptions) as a way of life - just how things are, (to be only 75% productive). Most in management therefore will continue to assume these things and do nothing. Organizational improvement can never really sustainably happen. Most just believe in the management myth that 'PEOPLE WILL BE PEOPLE, NOTHING TO REALLY DO ABOUT IT'.

DISCUSSION: UH HUH! ☺ ☹, ...well there's always pizza, giveaways, comp-time, picnics, cheese and fish programs, short-term fixes, gimmicks...

Let's talk gang...your thoughts? We are going to really change us, not do programs and gimmicks.

TALK #15 THINKING:

- ❖ **Takeaways**

- ❖ **Issues I need to think through and discuss with mentors**

- ❖ **What did Booker really intend here**

- ❖ **What do I want to add**

- ❖ **What are my concerns with this topic**

- ❖ **What might I need to discuss with my leader/boss?**

16

MY WAY, NOT MY WAY

(WHO ME?)

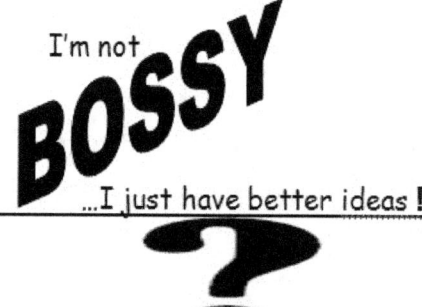

DISCUSSION: What do you think about when I mention the word Diversity?

<u>There is an angle of this diversity-thing that I have as part of my work always. There is something in my own recent experiences causing me to want to share it with you here.</u>

DISCUSSION: Diversity is normally connected with such things as gender, race and our differences in many respects. Likely you have had HR (Human Resources) presentations or mandatory trainings suggesting such things.

Leaders demonstrate and impose *diversity* on others in much more subtle ways. Its impact is just as serious as any of the other forms of diversity, when not understood.

I call this the 'My Way' factor, and it has serious consequences to our relationships. It is all something that needs embracing, understanding, awareness and for groups of people (teams to discuss. It can have a very serious impact on our ability to relate, get along, solve problems, make team-decisions and in general - work/play together...

<u>This aspect of diversity is very relevant to all of us who deal with people (which is just about all of us huh☺?)</u>

DISCUSSION: Each of us deals with this in many (likely all) phases of our lives: work, home, family, and I assume any relationship with others.

<u>I contend this to be a super-duper-especially-important dynamic for those in leadership/management roles. Leaders have the power to impose their 'Way' on subordinates; consciously or unconsciously.</u>

<u>Listen up leaders at all levels: this may be another one of those real 'KEYS TO YOUR SUCCESS'!!!</u>

DISCUSSION: This is a human-relations concept that we all know and realize to some degree. Maybe we just figure it is something that *others* do, but not YOU (me)!?!

The 'My Way' factor, in its simplest form is just the dynamic of wanting things done in the way that YOU would do them or want them done. It is purely natural, normal and maybe even logical. We all do have our own style of DOING everything & anything - based on our experiences, knowledge, upbringing, past role models, values, beliefs, and etcetera. We all see things from our own world's experience, and to some extent - all believe that your 'My Way' is THE BEST WAY.

Consider these aspects of the 'My Way' factor as we ponder this whole thing and try to determine how it impacts us in our relationships. We need awareness as well as how it impacts those that we lead or work with, etc.

<u>Let me attempt this by asking you to just consider how you differ from others, in the areas listed below? How do you deal with others who do not do it 'YOUR WAY'? Do you consider them not right...wrong even? ...frustrating? ...not as good? ...try to change them?</u>

KNOWINGLY LEADING!

<u>And subsequently, try to impose your 'My Way' standard on others, hummmmmmmmmmmmmm?</u>

DISCUSSION: Let's look at these few dynamics of individual behavior we all practice differently. Let's discuss these individually:

- **Work ethic:** How we approach our daily routine & projects? Do others go a hundred miles per hour like you? Are they crashing around, constantly appearing busy, or are they more methodical / laid-back in their approach? Which is right☺? ...are they 'DOING' something every minute, or taking time to process, ponder, think...? Do they take more breaks than you do?

- **Standards of housekeeping, Neat-ness:** In our offices, our cubes, our homes, and our dress/attire? In our work areas? Neat freak, or....? You into clutter or does it drive you crazy?

- **Communicating & relating:** Do they talk to others? Are you outgoing or a recluse? What does the team need from us? Does he/she pester and bother others or not say anything typically? Do they never add anything to conversations? Relational skills, thinking, behaviors, etc...? Does anyone talk constantly; you?

- **Handling of worries:** Emotions, the problems we are dealing with, at work or in personal lives? Bother others or keep everything to themselves....? Personal problems OK at work or not?

- **Tackling a problem:** We take our logic, experiences, beliefs, assumptions, and etc; then come up with THE answer! Do we have to be right? Do we consult/involve others? Not say anything until nearly too late? Are you a problem solver, decisive, apathetic...? How do you address problems; procrastinator?

- **Our pace or approach to work scheduling, prioritizing, doing first things first:** I read something a while back, which suggested the most challenging aspects of managing people is to LISTEN to them, and to GET THEM to do things in the right priority! Do others do stuff the way you would...? Are members of the team addressing things in the same (right) priority?

- **Expectations and standards with everything:** Work performance, goals, projects, etcetera? Are they clear, understood and agreed upon by both sides of the relationship? Are they realistic? Are we asking for perfection, when excellence is OK? And, come on, do you really need it NOW..........? ☺

TALK #16 THINKING:

- ❖ **Takeaways**

- ❖ **Issues I need to think through and discuss with mentors**

- ❖ **What did Booker really intend here**

- ❖ **What do I want to add**

- ❖ **What are my concerns with this topic**

- ❖ **What might I need to discuss with my leader/boss?**

17

CONSENSUS THINKING

(ALL MEANS ALL - DOESN'T IT?)

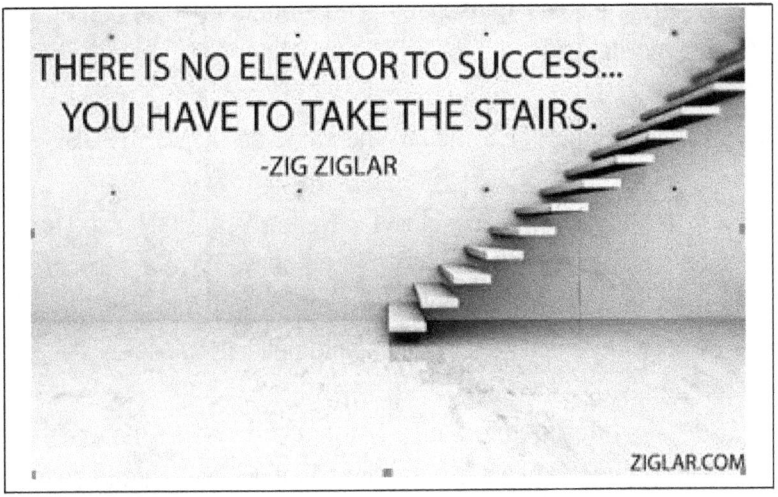

DISCUSSION: CONSENSUS - what is this term all about? Is it just another management fad; one which has come and gone never to be truly utilized or understood.

CONSENT, CENSUS, US???....these deriviations of this word may give us some hint of its meaning to teams, organizations or any entity needing to make decisions.

<u>Many leaders have never dealt with consensus; never had it modeled, and therefore don't really understand the dynamics. Trust me, some have never even heard of it!</u>

<u>I strongly recommend you think through this concept; maybe do some studying/reading on it. Feel free to holler at me as well.</u>

DISCUSSION: Let's talk through the what, why and hows regarding practicing 'consensus' as a team; and how I can and should facilitate it?

- ❖ MAJORITY RULES…is this the same as CONSENSUS?

    IF we buy into Majority Rules….we are very likely going to be satisfied with voting and as long as we have a majority, then we have a decision! The problem with this is that where there is a majority, this automatically implies a minority.
    We have therefore only winners and losers – not Consensus! Losers are the ones that will be heard to say later, "I told you so,……I knew it wouldn't work, and other such remarks". Even worse if we lost in the vote, we might work to ensure it fails (YOU would never do this would you?) This is all a clear indicator of no consensus from the beginning. Why?....because we did not practice consensus-seeking, we just looked for 'Majority Rules'.

- ❖ DEMOCRACY….This is closely aligned to the Majority Rules dynamics. Managers and Supervisors might fall into this same trap, thinking we are going to *be a democracy*. We will just do and respect what *most of us* want?! Sounds

KNOWINGLY LEADING!

good, but as we explained in the above paragraph about Majority Rules....

❖ BUY-IN.... What does this term mean? Consider the word BUY; what does it mean and when do we BUY? We buy when we can see the resulting value (purchase?) is worth the commitment of resources. This is what the buy-in concept is all about; and why it is so critical and not just another buzzword to toss around. We have bought in to the solution, understand it and can support in its execution.

<u>Consensus comes about when we all have the ability to discuss, hear, input, see and understand the solution; and therefore support it in execution.</u>

<u>Consensus happens when reasoning happens and when we understand others, as well as being understood.</u>

DISCUSSION: Let's talk through some pieces and parts of this Consensus-thing.

- ✓ TIME is potentially the biggest killer to the Consensus process. Doing it (consensus-seeking) takes time. Majority Rules and Dictatorship is much quicker!?!?!

- ✓ Do we truly understand the value and are we committed its importance, that we are willing to take the time to let the process work? What's the cost when we don't?

Facilitation Keys to Success:

- The problem is stated and clearly identified
- The leader does not state his/her opinion up front – just do YOUR job, facilitation
- Non threatening environment must be created, (possibly ground rules laid out)
- ALL opinions/thoughts/ideas are stated and clearly vocalized; and processed
- All ideas are valid and not to be abused
- Find ways to get those quiet people's ideas out there first
- Everyone is heard
- The solution (even if your idea didn't win) is understood and supportable
- WINNING and LOSING are concepts that go away... We are just after the BEST ANSWER!

✓ Fear of making it worse?

<u>Leaders go last, if at all...meaning that the leader is the process leader (the consensus process). When the leader is determined to impose his/her viewpoints and solutions up front or during the discussion, the process is likely going to be compromised and/or biased. One of the reasons why supervisors/managers typically</u>

KNOWINGLY LEADING!

<u>don't make good consensus-process leaders………because they do have a dog in the hunt.</u>
<u>They do care about which option is chosen and do have expertise in the area we are dealing with…</u>

<u>It is why facilitators outside of the area of concern have much better capability to facilitate the process with integrity; in an unbiased manner. This is because he/she does not care about the outcome---- but rather cares about the process.</u>

DISCUSSION:

- ✓ Attacking doesn't happen; we attack the problem vs each other

- ✓ When we succeed with consensus-seeking as our way of problem-solving and decision-making, then we:

ALL THINK
ALL LEARN
ALL UNDERSTAND
ALL REASON
ALL BUY-IN
ALL can SUPPORT
ALL GROW

….we **ALL** have the best answer!

TALK #17 THINKING:

❖ **Takeaways**

❖ **Issues I need to think through and discuss with mentors**

❖ **What did Booker really intend here**

❖ **What do I want to add**

❖ **What are my concerns with this topic**

❖ **What might I need to discuss with my leader/boss?**

18

TURNOVER REALITY

(IT'S ABOUT YOU, NOT THEM)

For the Small Business Owner (SBO) as well as the large corporation - *hiring and firing* people (turnover) hurts in a wide variety of ways. There is nothing new about that, although rarely is the root cause really defined and admitted. Most in management, would leap first to the 'hiring the wrong person' way of thinking; this is frequently not the actual cause (of them going away).

With all the efforts put into hiring, this just can't be the major issue here. After all, organizations are doing a lot of wringing their hands over making the decision who to hire – which is indeed smart!

<u>This hiring process can take weeks and even months; and may include assessments, personality profiling, testing, stressing, and multiple interviews. So hiring the wrong person is likely only a small piece of problem.</u>

DISCUSSION: The 'problem' here is in many (maybe most) cases, about the leader's failure of dealing with this fresh, enthusiastic, ready-to-go newbie/employee! This failure sometimes begins as soon as the employee is hired in...

Obviously this (turnover/people leaving) also happens to employees already on the team - after some period of time has passed in the employee's tenure. Leadership is failing to provide routine/frequent feedback (especially in the beginning). Instead, leadership just assumes it's about the new hire.

Here's a sample case-study I want to share and discuss with you guys:

[....Rodney, SBO, is doing well and has his business growing, and decides he needs an Assistant (or another body) to help out in his small service-oriented business. Rodney has taken nearly two months speaking to several potential new hires. Lots of deliberation occurs before finally taking the plunge and hiring Rachael. Rodney and his one other partner are ecstatic about what all Rachael is doing in the initial days/weeks. Everyone is 'happy' – the honeymoon is on...

Seemingly with very little guidance, she is just 'being everything that we hoped for, and MORE'. However some little things in Rachael's way of performing duties begins to irritate Rodney.

<u>*Likely there are some of those 'MY WAY' dynamics playing out here; for more on this, see Chapter 16.</u>

DISCUSSION: No big deal, so nothing is said …but the small issues grow.

Everyone knows about the issues (partners, family, friends, etc), except for Rachael of course! Rodney subconsciously believes it will just take care of itself, so Rodney does nothing (except bellyache to others about her).

Days and weeks go by and this boss/employee relationship erodes slowly; communication becomes challenging, avoiding talking happens, etc (you get the picture huh?). Rachael is feeling a bit uneasy but just assumes that if something were wrong, surely the boss would tell her! She even inquires now and then, only to receive a simple, 'all is fine'. Rodney and the partner converse about it and continue to be frustrated, and start thinking "well let's give her a couple of weeks and if nothing changes, well.…"

One day Rachael makes a mistake totally disconnected to the previous issue, and Rodney jumps on her big time for this error. Rachael is upset and has no clue why this was such a big deal. Yeah she made a mistake but did it necessitate all this ranting and raving? Five months and twenty-three days from the day she was hired, Rachael is let go. Bad feelings are felt on both sides, but "oh well", Rodney thinks, "It's just hard to find good help."

He, his partner, family and friends think and assume maybe the next one will work out...]

TURNOVER is alive and well here.

Across town, (in a large company with hundreds of employees) the HR Manager has just hired a new employee after several weeks of interviewing prospects. The new hire works out fine for a while, but is let go somewhere down the line – some kind of personality conflict he was having with the Supervisor. It's not real clear what happened, they just didn't work out.

Nothing different here except the corporation has the budget to do a lot more elaborate assessing/profiling before hiring of the 'right person' the next time! We better ramp up our hiring procedures, because that's the problem right? ☺

Supervisor and HR Manager look at each other, shaking their heads and muttering how difficult it is to find good people! It appears TURNOVER is alive and well here also

I think we have uncovered the root cause here: LEADERSHIP (not providing direction/feedback) is the issue vs. the hiring issue.

> [By the way, I do realize there is always the possibility that it was a 'wrong-hire'!!!? Maybe 2% of the time.]

DISCUSSION: So what are the messages and/or learning here for us?

How do we all make sure this doesn't happen to us, you guys, each of you?

How do I make sure it doesn't happen to me, between my boss and me?

For in-depth information on 'how to' implement a solid and sustainable evaluation and assessment process, see Chapter 14.

TALK #18 THINKING:

- ❖ *Takeaways*

- ❖ *Issues I need to think through and discuss with mentors*

- ❖ *What did Booker really intend here*

- ❖ *What do I want to add*

- ❖ *What are my concerns with this topic*

- ❖ *What might I need to discuss with my leader/boss?*

19

CHANGE FRUSTRATION

(OTHERWISE KNOWN AS CONTINUOUS IMPROVEMENT)

CHANGE

IS GOOD

...you go first!

DISCUSSION: We all know it to be a fact of life - all organizations deal with changes. By the way, that's a positive; because if we're not changing we can't be improving, right?

Let's think about how most people (maybe even you) typically respond to this question: Why do people react negatively to change?

The typical/normal 'dribble' answer and Management Myth is "blah, blah, blah....people just resist change naturally."

HOGWASH, I say...they resist change for very good and valid rationalizations that have come from their (our) previous experiences.

Let's take into consideration these three factors that lead to people's 'natural' resistance to change:

1) People perceive that we are **trying to change them** vs the process...

2) People don't like to be surprised (the **surprise** factor)...and

3) **People having no part** in the development of the change. Let's look at each just a bit...!

1) Continuous improvement, which we all agree is good and necessary, has one pretty predictable dynamic attached to it - change must occur. We must understand that although it may be our intent to change a system or process, people likely will take it as you trying to change them. People really have no other choice, you see, they are joined to that process for the moment. It is personal.

Most will be unable to separate themselves from the improvement of a process; unless it is carefully communicated to them. And, oh yeah, that would have happened except that we forgot to consult and involve them. Therefore the change came as a big surprise which we want them to just blindly accept and begin doing tomorrow morning!

2) The SURPRISE factor. Think for a moment, what is the normal evolution of a change in your organization? See if this has a familiar ring to it?

At some level an idea starts to brew...management takes charge...meetings begin to occur...lots of discussion, listening, reasoning, and understanding of the different points of view.

Of course, only the execs or 'management types' attend these meetings because we cannot interrupt those doing the work - production, services, daily operations, etc. Slowly, *we (management)* begin to digest the idea (change). It is accepted by all the key players and a decision is born! ...maybe over weeks, months, etc. Now it is time to take it to the floor and see what *they* think? (Like it really matters at this point, right?)

You see where this is going huh? Surprise, look at what we are going to do!

3) NO OWNERSHIP, buy-in....OR SUPPORT! "What's happening here? We've brought this to you (the employees) and it's a great idea! Trust us, we have thought this through from every possible angle...it's the best thing since sliced bread—it will work!"

*Let me assure you right now, it may work and could be a great idea.

It will only happen (because of how management did this) after a whole lot of wasted time, stress, arguing, hammering each other (and maybe each other's mothers), hurt feelings, damaged relations, explaining, etc.

DISCUSSION: The almost comical part of this is that again, it might have been a very good idea. The way we implemented IT made it needlessly painful! ...and took forever to get buy-in!

Management mumbles, "People will be people. People these days just don't accept change very well do they? People just naturally resist change, nothing you can do about it!"

When will we ever learn these lessons and quit doing this to the people and to the organization over and over again?

DISCUSSION: How can we ensure we do this right here on this team? Let's talk this out. Any thoughts? Let's discuss this. How do we make sure I (your leader) never reinforce these bad ways/habits of implementing changes?

KNOWINGLY LEADING!

Boy, Now let us GET REAL…people haven't changed much…they've always wanted to know WHY and be involved, right? Didn't you …don't you now???!

Some further thought on this change dynamic for you to ponder (or to actually share and directly converse about with your team.

Well regardless, it seems to be a 'toughie' for organizations, worth processing a bit (actually it is something I ponder quite a bit), so let's process!

The key it seems is merely for the organizational leadership to recognize and understand 'human behavior and people' — which we all know IS a challenge in itself.

The difficulty is that the people-dynamic is just not highly considered and understood, nor it's impact! Therefore, CHANGE frequently is very painful, wasteful, costly and destructive on a variety of levels.

FYI, there are plenty of Change Management (CM) models available; one only needs to do a Google-search and dozens will appear. However, even though communication and involving people is typically within most models, it's significance receives little focus. Some simply interpret and focus on communicating with the masses by a memo or speech by the Organizational Leader, announcing a great change being rolled out……

Yeah, that's communication, huh?

DISCUSSION: Here are some pieces of the change process I want to discuss and hammer around with you. These are big-picture at the organizational level, but I want to talk through them and their implication to us right here ...and my leadership?

- ✓ During the beginning phases managers are deliberating, argueing, going to meetings, discussing and otherwise accepting of the change. This is the time to also take it to the people for their reactions and input, not to mention it is allowing them to begin accepting, processing, etc.

- ✓ Every step of the way, ask people about what they think?...why it won't work in their minds...

- ✓ Ensure that from start-to-finish, that the 'surprise' factor is never possible with anyone...

- ✓ Involve / gain input from all within the organization, even the custodian, who will have some connection to the change...

- ✓ ...and don't forget Ol Bob, 'the pain in the butt, difficult, negative and challenging guy that he is'. You know that ONE we want to leave out of the talks - is the one that will show up later at implementation time (likely with some real valid issues we didn't consider). We will pay for it... (None of us would do this, humm? ☺).

- ✓ We must not fall into the trap of the thinking, "we can't bother the people, they are too busy making product, providing our services and bottom line, being productive." After all only managers have time for meetings/talks....

- ✓ Buy-in is gained from top to bottom, every phase of the CM process...before we move on, ALL agree...

- ✓ Leaders, (managers, supervisors) must accept the change before we move on to the troops. Frequently organizations do not even ensure that the leadership is bought-in! This is not a good thing; after all, they are the ones who are to be facilitating the change at their level...

- ✓ Don't forget to inquire/consult with ALL customers - Internal and External. All that the change can and will touch...

TALK #19 THINKING:

- *Takeaways*

- *Issues I need to think through and discuss with mentors*

- *What did Booker really intend here*

- *What do I want to add*

- *What are my concerns with this topic*

- *What might I need to discuss with my leader/boss?*

20

CONFLICT BASICS

(I'M RIGHT, YOU'RE WRONG...
...YOU'RE RIGHT AS LONG AS YOU AGREE WITH ME)

DISCUSSION: Conflict is obviously a reality and huge aspect present anywhere that people function together. It is a part of organizational culture and a challenge within the management world. So let me share with you some concerns, observations and teachings that I have realized over the last several years as a leader and follower.

People will be in conflict, accept it, it is a fact… the only ingredients required = people 'working together'.

The issue may be anything, from implementing a new program to exactly where we should place a wastebasket! Maybe the most significant takeaway I could share with you and want us to embrace is this one: just because people oppose your thought, idea or way of doing something, doesn't make them an enemy!

This seems obvious, but trust me, we all have a tendency to 'go there' when we face another's perspective or someone's opposing point of view. This is especially true when relationships are not strong; another reason I am being so persistent with this topic!

Let's stop this practice of 'opposing opposing thought' and change our way of thinking on our team!

Let's consider some realities here. We work with people that we did not (or would not) likely have chosen – if it had been our choice. Unlike other situations, (like church, our school days and/or some other social setting where we get to choose those that we want to be with) – in the workplace it is rarely our decision who we get to 'play with'. In those previous situations in life, we can walk away at any time; it is not the same in the work environment. Therefore, you must get along with others or face conflict….or leave, (which rarely seems to be a good option)?!?

One source that I came across a while back, posed the following ideas about organizational conflict. It said: Conflict between people(s) can probably be broken down into one of two categories: Personality or Job-related.

Although we all tend to jump to the conclusion that any opposition means there is a personality conflict present, that is normally not the case. More often than not, it is more a matter of something within the job structure or organizational dynamics - that is placing people into conflict. Here are a few of the possibilities caused by organizational dynamics:

"... different expectations, sharing of resources, unclear reporting structure, overlapping roles or job functions, differences in standards, unclear expectations, lack of consistent accountability, my manager not liking your manager, etc..."

To expand on this just a bit, consider this case-study/scenario:

Picture this - Five co-workers having to utilize three computers. The organization just figures that this should work and the number of computers ought to be enough. The assumption is made that the people will share appropriately and fairly (play well together). You and I know this is not always the case. Another dynamic that does seem to be prevalent and cause significant conflict as well is the 'only one right answer mentality'.

We all possess this mentality to some degree. I will phrase it in a couple of different ways: "You are right as long as you agree with me..." (or) "I'm right, therefore you must be wrong".

Here is a little leadership perspective - we leaders tend at times, to not deal with conflict for some of the following reasons: it is personal - not my business...they will work it out... I don't have the tools to facilitate resolution... fear of taking sides - judging one over the other... I will just make it worse, or ... I don't have time to mess with it.

The reality is that we must deal with conflicts. For the record, it is ALWAYS the leader's (my) business! Why? How? Because people in conflict, to some degree affect some or all of the following: productivity, teamwork, communication, relationships, morale.. Need I say more?

There are many models out there to deal with conflict resolution. Let me just offer here a couple of concepts that need to be part of whatever model you utilize:

1) They must be forced to listen to each other (yes, you can force listening!).

2) Buy-in must be part of the solution, in other words, it cannot be your solution, but one that THEY develop.

3) Accountability must be present, WE WILL come back together to review the success of the solution.

A final thought regarding 'not having time' to deal with it - Take the time now or you will spend much more time later (pay me now or pay me later).

> "...You have heard, 'Love your neighbor, and hate your enemies'. But I tell you, 'Love your enemies and pray for those who persecute you... If you love those who love you, what reward will you get? Even the tax collectors do that; and if you greet only your brothers, what are you doing better/more than others?" MATTHEW 5:43

This scripture has particular significance to all of us in the workplace (as well as every part of our lives huh?) This reminds me of something I wrote a few years ago regarding working with 'others'. The article focused on the challenge of working with those we don't get along with - are in conflict with - or let's just say the relationship is less than good.

*Chapter 9 of this book discusses this OTHER-concept in more depth. (Some redundancy which I decided was a good thing)

Here are some Odds n Ends about Conflict & a Model to use in Facilitation:

Process these, understand and then speak to them in your discussions about conflict. (Please feel free to call on me if I can help with your processing...)

DISCUSSION: REASONS & RATIONALIZATIONS *why leaders don't get involved in conflict resolution:*

- don't like confrontation
- fear of taking sides
- no time to screw with it
- no tools (like this model)
- might take care of itself
- I might make it worse
- ???

I like this model below because it deals with the above rationalizations (IF you facilitate and stay out of it):

- time efficient,
- prevents leader from judging/taking sides,
- they solve their own problem,
- forces listening to happen, and
- Provides a tool to the leader....

[Keeping it simple, here's a scenario: Bob and Sally have to share one computer, heated emotional conflict going on, not sharing/playing well together ☺]

Facilitator follows these 'problem-solving' steps; ONLY facilitating, not inputting...:

KNOWINGLY LEADING!

Let me walk and talk us through a model I came across a long time ago (no idea where!?!??). I want us to consider using going forward:

1) Bob states the problem as Bob sees / thinks it...
2) Sally 'repeats' what Bob has said, not agrees, but repeats
3) Bob concurs that Sally has it (his thinking), or not....if not, return to #1

4) Sally states...
5) Bob repeats...
6) Sally concurs...

(Thru Step 6 we have only ID (d) the problem to each other & forced listening – HUGE)

7) Discussion, search of Alternatives/Options...
8) Agreement on something, Bob takes computer in morning, Sally in PM
9) Accountability Step: Agreement to all return soon, next few days and discuss how the agreement is working........or start over.
10) Go try it.

11) Do #9, and don't forget to come back together to ensure it is all really solved, or not!

TALK #20 THINKING:

❖ **Takeaways**

❖ **Issues I need to think through and discuss with mentors**

❖ **What did Booker really intend here**

❖ **What do I want to add**

❖ **What are my concerns with this topic**

❖ **What might I need to discuss with my leader/boss?**

21

ISSUES WITH YOU

(WHO'S THE MESSAGE FOR ANYWAY?)

DISCUSSION: Here's a dynamic we have all experienced with teams, groups, departments and/or organizations.

COMMUNICATING MESSAGES (ISSUES) TO THE WRONG PERSON!

*Write this (above) on the whiteboard maybe...

*Please read all this through carefully a couple of times, because it's relevant to every one of us—we've all seen it...done it...and had it 'done' to us as well! This goes on all the time, but if your team can get hold of this one…enormous strides can be made in increased:

- ✓ teamwork,
- ✓ trust,
- ✓ less conflict,
- ✓ more productivity and
- ✓ Improved relationships all the way around.

DISCUSSION: Look at what I wrote up here on the board. Any thoughts what that's about? This is a topic that can potentially tear apart people, relationships and teams. Here's a scenario to help us discuss this:

*This topic closely ties to other chapters here such as the ones on TURNOVER, CONFLICT, etc. This is great reinforcement of many of the same principles and values we are after here.

DISCUSSION: Situation: You have a problem with someone (what they said, what you thought they said, their opinion, something they did that impacted your world, etc. Get the picture?)

What do we typically do when this occurs? We go share it with someone else—a peer, a boss, spouse; everyone except the person who really needs to hear it! [Starting to connect aren't you...?]

Teammates (employees within the same office-under the same leader) frequently may even take it straight to the leader for him/her to deal with...

Let's think through the impact and fallout of doing things this way -- first of all the person you are taking it to can do nothing but listen to you bellyache. What are you (we) expecting them to do with it? If they go do something with it, then they have broken your trust!?! If you allow them (or push them to do it for you) - all you are going to do is lose respect and your relationship with that individual big time!

Teams (like us) have to honestly sit down, look each other in the eye and say "we all have our gripes with each other at times; how do we want to deal with it?"

Well? Let's take issues and problems to the person in question. This is all obviously closely tied to gossiping – that's for sure one we don't want here on our team.

After all, if you tell me (the culprit ☺) what your issue is or what you don't like that I did or whatever, haven't you actually done something positive regarding our relationship and the team overall? But we tend to take confrontation and disagreement as world-shattering stuff instead of the good that is to be gained?

If we can manage to do it in a respectful, tactful and non-confrontational way; it can drastically improve our team in ways we cannot even imagine. Much of this is tied closely to our discussions regarding conflict huh?

Consider this: Conflict can be a good thing, but only if dealt with and resolved?

Failing to 'message the right person' tears down relationships, discourages communication, kills trust and makes life miserable for all around the issue. Not to mention all the wasted time that these kind of things end up taking; because we took it through a cycle and circle of 'the wrong people'.

<u>As Leaders, Mentors, Friends and Co-workers – we can help others by steering them in the right direction (to the right person vs the wrong person – YOU!) Maybe give them first a few moments of empathetic listening?!?</u>

<u>Hopefully they will send you away the first time you screw this up as well.</u>

TALK #21 THINKING:

- **Takeaways**

- **Issues I need to think through and discuss with mentors**

- **What did Booker really intend here**

- **What do I want to add**

- **What are my concerns with this topic**

- **What might I need to discuss with my leader/boss?**

22

'FINE LINE' RELATIONS

(HEALTHY RELATIONSHIPS CANNOT BE TOO STRONG)

DISCUSSION: Consider this list of phrases most managers have heard from somewhere. By the way, I want to NOT be what I am describing here:

"don't get too close,
...maintain that fine line between you & your people,
...keep your distance,
...you can't be a friend & a boss..."

These are commonly spoken and widely accepted 'management myths' heard when people speak of the workplace and a manager's relationship with his/her people.

Managers say these things and therefore just maintain the status quo. We are just maintaining vs continuously improving (relationships) when we think this way!

<u>Ponder that for a moment.</u>

DISCUSSION: Real Leaders (which I'm trying to be here) attempt to grow, build & improve these relationships as close as possible! I know my success depends on the quality of my relationship with each of you; I have no doubt about this.

What do you think about all this? I am sure many and maybe most of you have had some bad experiences with bosses who got too close, made no effort, played favorites, etc. What are your thoughts about how our relationships should BE?

<u>Because so many people have experienced manager's abusing their authority, relations and position, it has come to be a myth widely touted in management circles. It is found in management-theory courses and most anyplace you see management taught.</u>

DISCUSSION: Not 'here' my friend; I don't buy it for a second – I'm going to practice LEADERSHIP & RELATIONSHIP!

<u>I believe this mentality of 'not getting to close' comes from managers who practiced (or had practiced on them): favoritism, abused their roles, not holding all equally accountable, taking advantage of people, promoting on friendship, etc.</u>

<u>These are ill-equipped managers who screwed up the relationship; didn't have any self-awareness or discipline, etc…</u>

<u>If you are a leader or trying to become one, realize this – your success is going to come from them (your people). What kind of leader would YOU perform for the best? What kinds of leader have YOU worked for the most effectively?</u>

<u>Of course the answer is the one you had the best relationship with, right? We speak of the importance of relationships among team-members and how dysfunctional teams are when relationships aren't good; but the leader needs to keep his/her distance?!?</u>

DISCUSSION: We won't fall into this way of thinking; I intend to work on developing relationships with you all as tight as possible. When we create comfort, trust, respect, great communications and a desire for people to want to be here with YOU and the others……great things happen!

KNOWINGLY LEADING!

The result is awesome productivity, loyalty, low turnover and believe it or not - people looking forward to coming to work. When the leader cares about his/her folks; is there for them outside their job; wants to support and help them with troubles; and even socializes with them AFTER work, etc – now we have a great family-like relationship.

I am betting some of you don't see this; don't believe we should even consider things like socializing together. Nobody is right or wrong here. This is a personal choice between each of us, but let's discuss and ensure we are all comfortable where we are going?

> Now of course, there can be issues and risks, but not if YOU the leader do things right! If fair expectations and accountability happen with everyone, these issues don't exist! The problem is NOT about this 'buddy & boss' concept & debate, it's about YOU the leader, and your leadership! I have indeed worked with and coached great leaders who would not go there as I am describing! They maintained this 'fine line' and wouldn't let the relationship exist outside the workplace. It's just my opinion they were limiting themselves & the potential of this relationship.

DISCUSSION: Let's discuss the risks and why some leaders (and followers) don't *GO THERE*!?! Have you seen relationship issues along these lines? Let's learn from each other's bad experiences...and good ones?

Jesus broke bread and spent countless hours teaching, socializing & continuously improving the relationships with those he led. The Word (bible) speaks to developing a personal relationship with Him. How about between us?

Shouldn't the ULTIMATE LEADER's leadership style be our guide?

TALK #22 THINKING:

- ❖ **Takeaways**

- ❖ **Issues I need to think through and discuss with mentors**

- ❖ **What did Booker really intend here**

- ❖ **What do I want to add**

- ❖ **What are my concerns with this topic**

- ❖ **What might I need to discuss with my leader/boss?**

23

BAD APPLE MYTH

(WHAT WE EXPECT, WE GET)

> *"...When they saw Jesus having dinners with tax collectors & 'sinners', they asked his disciples "Why does your teacher eat with tax collectors & 'sinners'?" On hearing this, Jesus said, "It is not the healthy who need a doctor, but the sick. But go & learn what this means....For I have not come to call the righteous, but sinners & the sick..."*
>
> MATT 9:11-13

DISCUSSION: There are so many messages within these scriptures for leaders (and for me), but allow me to focus on one specific message I want to relate to and use in our discussions here at this moment.

KNOWINGLY LEADING!

<u>Here is an assumption from my first book, 'Teaching Fishing':</u>

<u>Both leaders and followers in the workplace and in society have become accepting and numb to ineffective leadership. Most of us have accepted how non-productive, unenthusiastic, uninspiring and ineffective we and those around us really are! We accept this 'lack' as just the way it is and how it has to be (poor relationships between individuals and departments ...conflicts ...bottlenecks ...poor attitudes... bad apples and ...bad management).]</u>

<u>After all, people will be people (Another management myth by managers not knowing how to lead - big time crappola)</u>

DISCUSSION: I want to share some thinking I have embraced, learned from someone years back. The point I am going to be pursuing here is regarding what I call the 'bad apples' myth. This obviously ties to our BOTTLENECK and OTHERS concept we spoke to earlier. Let me just talk to the point as I had it shared with me and then we'll discuss...

There is this conscious or subconscious thinking on the part of many in leadership roles (and among people on teams as well); that there just will always be those 'couple of bad apples' on every team. These bad apples might be viewed as the one, two or three folks on every team that have issues,... personal life issues,... cause trouble,... they are challengers of everything,... don't seem to be team-players,... the ones always in conflict,... have a habit that drives others crazy, ... Or some other shortage of abilities, common sense and/or skills.

You are thinking about others right now aren't you? Well maybe you are a bad apple? Ever think of that?

In looking back at the scripture, Jesus speaks of His role to teach or serve those who NEED (leadership), healing or teaching! The righteous and/or healthy ones, (that other 80-90%) the *easy* members of your team are not who need your leadership - it's the bad apples.

Leaders tend to take credit for the ones (the 80-90%) who are healthy and play well on the team. Then they use the 'bad apple' logic/language to avoid their (the leader's) job, their actual and real LEADERSHIP CHALLENGE!?! They are rationalizing away their role in leading others out of the bad apple kingdom. Those few are just helpless; what's this say about the leadership?

As leaders, we likely have a high percentage of folks who are just fine with or without my leadership; could probably work for any knucklehead manager actually. My responsibility and role on the team (if I am to be an effective leader vs just another manager maintaining status quo) is to teach, lead, grow, mentor and develop those sick ones...the bad apples.

<u>To reiterate here: Managers & organizations often just view 'bad apples' as if they are unsalvageable and the only solution is to just get rid of them. While there is undoubtedly a small percentage that deserve this and need to be tossed out; the vast majority of those bad apples (in my humble opinion) can be 'led' to become healthy productive team players.</u>

<u>Are you up for your LEADERSHIP CHALLENGE? Are you willing to have 'dinners' with the sick (the bad apples); teach and make them well? Jesus knew his purpose ... do you, do we, and does organizational leadership?</u>

DISCUSSION: My intention here is to kill this myth and ensure we have zero bad apples at all times. This doesn't mean we all can't and won't be a BOTTLENECK now and then, but a 'bad apple' ...NO!

WHATCHATHINKIN'???

TALK #23 THINKING:

- ❖ **Takeaways**

- ❖ **Issues I need to think through and discuss with mentors**

- ❖ **What did Booker really intend here**

- ❖ **What do I want to add**

- ❖ **What are my concerns with this topic**

- ❖ **What might I need to discuss with my leader/boss?**

24

ROOT CAUSE, COMMUNICATIONS = RELATIONSHIPS

(AND VICE VERSA)

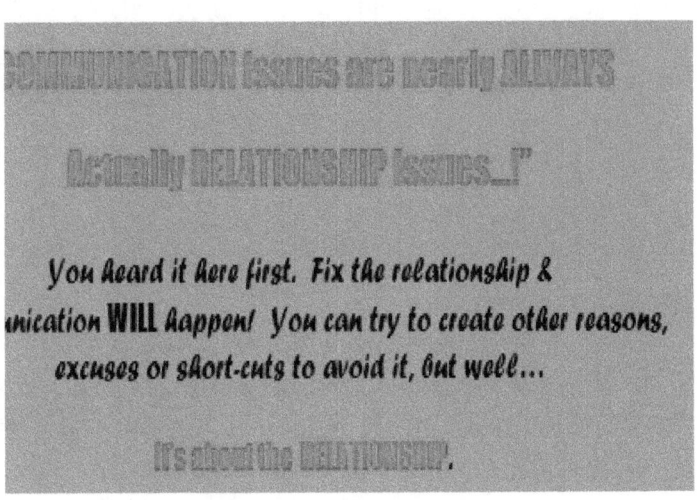

"COMMUNICATION issues are nearly ALWAYS actually RELATIONSHIP issues...!"

You heard it here first. Fix the relationship & communication WILL happen! You can try to create other reasons, excuses or short-cuts to avoid it, but well...

It's about the RELATIONSHIP.

<u>COMMUNICATION PROBLEMS</u>: This is always the *number one need* identified by organizations upon my initial contact / in my consultation practice.

Anyone and everyone tells me, "We need to be able to communicate more effectively".
Once again, I look at leadership as the primary answer to this challenge; ineffective leaders are typically the root cause.

In my initial years, I would fall into the trap of focusing on structure, bulletin boards, emailing procedures, org chart stuff, meetings, etc.
While all these are worth pondering, I now know that those were just symptoms and excuses vs the root cause – Bad RELATIONSHIPS!

DISCUSSION:

- How does the management staff (our company's chain of command) verbally communicate information in all directions?

- Do we rely on Human Resources (personnel office) to distribute information?

- Is it possible that we have become reliant on bulletin boards, memos, fax, texting, email, etc vs the verbal word?

- What are our communication processes and methods for information flow, suggestions, ideas, policy, etc?

- Do we know where the barriers exist? What are our barriers here within our team and externally as well?

- Is it possible that none of these dynamics are what we really struggle with?

- In all the cases we have just discussed or pointed out; is it a COMMUNICATION challenge you/we are facing, or actually a RELATIONSHIP issue?

- All of our discussions previously and many in the future will focus on our relationships heavily; this is one critical reason. If we don't relate, communication suffers. As I think of all those I personally struggle to communicate with (which includes some of you and some in upper authority roles), if I am being honest – it's about my relationship with that person.

- The relationship between our office/department and some others in our company is also worth realizing, discussing and fixing as well!

TALK #24 THINKING:

- ❖ *Takeaways*

- ❖ *Issues I need to think through and discuss with mentors*

- ❖ *What did Booker really intend here*

- ❖ *What do I want to add*

- ❖ *What are my concerns with this topic*

- ❖ *What might I need to discuss with my leader/boss?*

KNOWINGLY LEADING!

25

TOP 10 LIST

(WANTED: GREAT LEADERS!)

> **TREAT EMPLOYEES LIKE THEY MAKE A DIFFERENCE AND THEY WILL.**
> — Jim Goodnight, CEO, SAS

*This is intentionally the last talk to tie us back to the first talk!

This is a nice list (top 10 below) no doubt, at least it helps in leading you to the answer of: 'WHAT AM I SUPPOSED TO BE AS A LEADER?'

This is again about the vagueness of leadership and why it is untargeted in terms of changing and improving.

<u>There are lots of lists of the WHAT, but little of HOW TO. The vision created in talks #2 and #3 (of this book) helps us get closer to a list like the one here below... By pursuing these conversations we can have one directly applicable to your leadership and to those you are currently leading (or preparing to).</u>

'WITHOUT DIRECTION, WE WANDER'

<u>This may not be the most all-inclusive and perfect list, however I would surmise that if any leader routinely led according to these factors, they would be one darned-good leader in most follower's eyes!</u>

<u>And just a recommendation: add, delete, edit (and with your people), go create a better list, your list, their list!</u>

DISCUSSION: Here is a Top 10 list I came across years ago - as expressed by people in all kinds of organizations serving in all kinds of different capacities. I want us to discuss these, add some that may not be on this list and then continue to dialogue about these as they pertain to us. Let's work on and figure out how we can make me accountable to be this kind(s) of leader.

I want to also tie this back to our talk about VISION, LEADER QUALITIES, VALUES, etc.

You are going to be key in making me accountable...in helping me grow into becoming these!

- ❖ I WANT my boss to support me, shield me and care about me - not just care about what I can do as am employee. Feedback would be nice every now and then also.

- ❖ I WISH my boss would deal with that one person that makes everybody else miserable. That one 'bad apple' is just allowed to do what he wants, because you are afraid of him, or think that we can't live without him; what a joke.

- ❖ I WANT to be involved 'early on' regarding impending changes, new ideas, solutions to problems. When I am not involved, I just start not caring about how well things are done, get an attitude and become very apathetic. My motivation is shot.

- ❖ I NEED the opportunity to develop myself, be taught new skills, have the opportunity to be promoted, or maybe just be recognized for what I do now. I cannot do this (again) without feedback.

- ❖ I WISH things were done fairly, no matter who knows who, or who the boss likes at the moment.

- ❖ I WISH I could be communicated with on what is going on, not just what she thinks I need to know. I find more out more from co-workers than I do from above…

- ❖ I WANT conflict to be dealt with fairly, quickly and sustainably. When people are in conflict, it is just allowed to fester, drive everyone else crazy and puts everyone on edge. So much waste occurs during these screwed up relationships.

- ❖ I WISH we would take the time to do things right. We rush through everything; like when someone new is hired, we just give them a few minutes of training and throw them into the routine. We barely even introduce them, and for sure we are setting them up for failure, because of poor training. Team-building is basically non-existent.

- ❖ I NEED my boss to provide me the resources I need to do my job well.

- ❖ I WISH I was more challenged, maybe even get you to delegate some things to me. You are afraid to let anyone else do anything for fear of your own job, or maybe just doesn't trust anyone. How will we ever get any better?

KNOWINGLY LEADING!

<u>These 'wishes & wants' are necessary for you to flourish, grow, learn and become more and more productive and useful to THEM and to the ORGANIZATION.</u>

<u>Maybe the question is, are you modeling the right stuff? Is there a clear target on which you can focus?</u>

Apologizing does not always mean you are wrong, it just means that you value your relationships more than your ego.

TALK #25 THINKING:

- *Takeaways*

- *Issues I need to think through and discuss with mentors*

- *What did Booker really intend here*

- *What do I want to add*

- *What are my concerns with this topic*

- *What might I need to discuss with my leader/boss?*

WRAPPING THIS UP

Leadership is so undefined, under-developed and within our culture, IS our most wasted resource. I do not intend to get into the reasons, but it is true. This waste is such an immense cost to organizations (go read my first three books or call me and we can discuss).

Leadership is plain and simply _difficult_ and a skill rarely developed individually or collectively. It is my hope that what you just experienced here in these conversations will simplify it and make you one of the rare ones KNOWINGLY LEADING. Regardless of how effective you actually use these – if committed to and practiced, you will KNOWINGLY be LEADING (and in the top 15-20% of leaders is my bet).

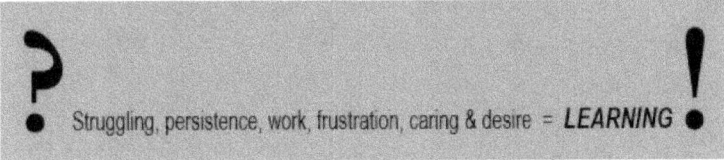
Struggling, persistence, work, frustration, caring & desire = **LEARNING**

I actually have no doubt this will be the case IF you sincerely try to do what is described, intended and laid out here. Seek coaching, mentors and accountability from others; find other resources to reinforce this learning.

Please also realize a major piece of what makes learning leadership so hard, is that very few of us have a real leader 'over us'. Therefore we are on our own, left to our own devices to find learning.

The learning I hope you really found here is the resource right under your nose – THEM (your people/team)! The ones you lead are the ones with which IF you have these conversations ...can and will grow you (and subsequently grow themselves).

Regarding your own boss, find ways (call me, I have ideas) to cause him/her to learn these dynamics as well. Your boss NOT knowing these concepts and NOT having these conversations, will harm you. Don't let that happen; teach, facilitate or what I call 'upward-coach' him/her.

Your survival and leadership success has nearly as much to do with *your leader* as with those you lead. Teach in all directions my friend. Learn, BE! ...then go teach.

A QUESTION FOR LEADERS (that's YOU right?)

Q: Are you influencing others or Are you being influenced by...? Are you conforming to the culture or Creating a culture?

I have one more piece of advice in YOU going forward with these conversations - research each before beginning the dialogue. These vignettes are intentionally brief, go do some googling on the topic and add reinforcing thoughts from other sources.

I have likely only given you a synopsis, only enough to raise awareness and get your THINKER thinking! Never stop thinking, growing you and them – continuously improving your world.

I do want to mention that these are my concepts and ideas; what I teach and preach in my business (www.bookertraining.com). I have many exercises, activities and role plays that I use in reinforcing these 'learnings'. Obviously if I can help you in facilitating some or all of this, call to discuss.

AUTHOR

President and Founder of Booker Training Associates; Doug is a Facilitator, Change Agent, Coach, Author & Leadership-Developer. Booker Training Associates is a business Doug began after a successful military career, retiring as a Major from the Army in 1992. The idea for his work evolved as Doug began realizing the 'challenge' facing organizations in managing (leading) people.

Ultimately he focuses on organizational & individual leadership behavior - helping not just the leader or manager, but with what he calls 'People-Systems'.

A strong believer in the need for continued learning, he has completed many certifications along with earning a Master's degree in Management. In his 20 years of serving organizations and individual leaders, Doug has worked with a variety of industries and also teaches in Higher Education with various universities. Along with his teaching and consulting work, he has now authored six books on Leadership, Personal Significance and Faith.

KNOWINGLY LEADING!

Doug regards his wife Sydney, two children, siblings and extended family as the best parts of his life. A close 2nd is being able to work in a field that he loves and considers his passion, and maybe even a ministry of sorts. All involves HELPING OTHERS - which is all that really matters.

While teaching at Kansas State University, Doug was selected as the Army's National Leadership Faculty of the Year in 1989; receiving this recognition from the Secretary of Defense in Washington D.C. Doug was also recently recognized as Faculty of the Year at Baker University in KC. He also teaches with Webster University and St Mary's University.

913.232.0244

29320 W 153 Terrace, Gardner Lake, KS 66030

Linked In & Facebook (Doug Booker),

Twitter (BookerTraining)

Email: doug@bookertraining.com

"I would love to hear from you regarding this book or any of my other books as well. Always open for a talk about Leadership, Relationships, Faith or YOU!' I always enjoy adding new quality people to my life; so let's talk! God's best my friend....."

KNOWINGLY LEADING!

Previous books:

Teaching Fishing for Managers, 2009 (republished 2013)

Rebuilding on Rock, 2010

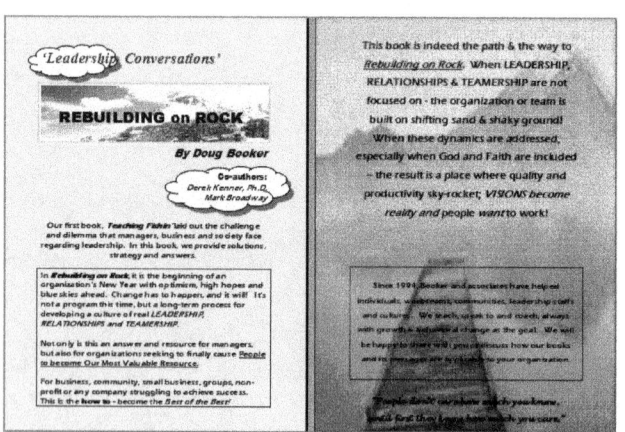

The Conference for Leaders, 2011

SIGNIFICANCE Starts Now – How We Live Our Lives Matters, 2012

Triangles, Compasses & GOD, 2013

*MY BOOKS CAN BE FOUND THROUGH MY WEBSITE (WWW.BOOKERTRAINING.COM) AS WELL AS ON AMAZON & KINDLE. YOU CAN ALWAYS CONTACT ME DIRECTLY FOR PURCHASING COPIES DIRECTLY. ASK ME FOR A FREE EBOOK/PDF VERSION!

<u>Let me write your story....</u> *Beginning in 2015 I am going to write your stories. This may be a biography or auto-biography; a story of success, a life of struggle, your parent's story or whatever your story is – that you wish to tell. I would be honored to do this with you.*

KNOWINGLY LEADING!

You CANNOT not 'LEAD BY EXAMPLE'!

(think about it...)

I would rather <u>see</u> a sermon
than <u>hear</u> one any day...

I'd rather you would walk with me,
than merely show the way...

The lectures you deliver
may be very wise and true,
but I think I'll get my lesson
by watching what you do...

Because I might misunderstand you,
and all the high advice you give,
but there's no misunderstanding
how you act and how you live.

We are ALWAYS 'LEADING BY EXAMPLE'

(Anonymous author, well said!)

www.ingramcontent.com/pod-product-compliance
Lightning Source LLC
Chambersburg PA
CBHW051803170526
45167CB00005B/1858